Messages of Hope

Words of Encouragement That Will Inspire, Lift Up, Challenge and Edify Your Spirit

By Dwayne Savaya

Dedication

I dedicate this book to my mother who is my angel on this earth. She is my strength, my support and my constant joy. Thank you mom for all that you have done for me.

I equally dedicate this book to my Lord and Savior Jesus Christ who has been my Rock, my Shield and my Inspiration. He guides my every word and without Him I would be nothing. Thank you Lord for allowing me to serve you.

To God belongs all the Glory, Honor and Praise for the great things He has done and continues to do through my life.

I recognize and acknowledge that it is "Not by might, nor by power, but by My Spirit saith the Lord." Zechariah 4:6

Epigraph

...God chose the foolish things of the world, that He might put to shame them that are wise; and God chose the weak things of the world, that He might put to shame the things that are strong...that no flesh should glory before God.

1 Corinthians 1:26-29 ASV

Table of Contents

Introduction

My name is Dwayne Savaya and this is my first book. I would like to share a little bit about myself in this introduction so that when you are reading my messages in this book you will understand who the writer is, what he has been through and how he can still have such a positive outlook on life. My story is not unlike many who have gone through terrible tragedies and setbacks and have come through them better, wiser and stronger than they were before, but my story and my messages don't focus on my own strength or ability or will to overcome, but rather I boast in the ability, in the strength, in the encouragement, in the sustenance, provision and leading of my Lord and Savior Jesus Christ who has been more faithful to me than I could ever be to Him.

In July of 1996 one month after my High School graduation and 11 days after my 18th birthday I suffered a spinal cord injury due to a boating accident that left me a quadriplegic. The C-5 and C-6 bones in my neck were shattered which bruised my spinal cord and left me paralyzed. As a result I have no movement from the chest down. I am unable to move my legs, my feet or my fingers. I do have limited mobility of my arms which allow me to work on a laptop computer and write my messages either using my index finger or my voice recognition software which allows me to write in a more fluid and natural manner. Of course I prefer the voice recognition software :-)

In 1999 one year after I gave my heart to the Lord, I prayerfully started God's Work Ministry with the website Godswork.org that was mainly focused on providing stories and poems that would encourage and inspire the reader to believe in themselves and to know that a new beginning was possible with God. The website became very popular just by word of mouth and many people contacted me to let me know they were encouraged, challenged and inspired by the messages they read. That encouraged my heart and a year after that in March of 2000 I started the God's Work Encouragement Mailing List where I would send encouraging and inspiring e-mail messages to people who subscribed through my website. Within a year the messages were going around the world to countries I had never even heard of. That was the power of e-mail. I also started a Prayer Ministry where members were able to send in prayer requests and have other e-mail members receive those requests and pray on their behalf. Many people were blessed by the prayer ministry and continue to be.

Becoming a writer was something that God inspired. I haven't had any training in any particular writing skills except what I learned in high school. I am not trained in biblical theology and I have not been to any seminary school though I wish I could have. I have studied the Word of God, read books by many preachers, but most importantly I have been sensitive to the leading of the Holy Spirit. The messages that I write are completely inspired by the Lord because I know I don't have the wisdom, the knowledge or the understanding to write such beautifully, articulate and thoughtful words of hope and encouragement. I pray as you read the messages, you will see and understand what I mean. And that is why I am quick to give God all the credit for every blessing that comes forth from this work. That is why my ministry is called God's Work. It is not my own and I do not claim any credit.

I do hope that the messages I have included in this book will be a great blessing to you and to those you may share them with.

I never thought or imagined my life would be used in this manner, but I am glad that God has found me worthy enough to be a part of His eternal work.

–Dwayne

How You Can Read This Book

The messages within this book have one main focus; to lift you up, to encourage, inspire and challenge you to become all that God has made you to be. This book has one basic theme, but each message stands on its own. You can pick any message and read it all on its own without worrying about missing a particular point in any other part of the book.

I have divided the messages into four categories for your convenience; Encouraging Messages, Inspiring Messages, Challenging Messages and Edifying Messages. You can select any of these categories or messages below the categories to go to that particular message.

Notes For The Reader

As you read the messages in this book I want you to see and know that at the end of most paragraphs I do have scriptures in parentheses that are there for your edification and verification of what was written. In my messages I never intend or assume to say anything without having the correct scripture references to back up what that message is trying to convey.

I would also encourage you to have your Bible next to you as you read the messages so that you can look up the Scriptures that I reference so that you may have a better understanding of the complete message.

My main emphasis for this book is for the reader to have clarity. I don't want any confusion when it comes to the Word of God and the Message of Hope that He offers to the world.

It is my hope and prayer that you will benefit from every message in this book. I pray that it will improve your outlook, that it will better your mindset, that it will encourage and inspire you to be all that God has made you to be.

–Dwayne

Encouraging Messages

The following messages are written to bring
encouragement to your heart knowing that a new
beginning is always possible with God despite our
shortfalls and our setbacks. We simply must allow
ourselves to begin again and have a deep knowing that our
crooked paths will be made straight.

Seeing Your Blessings

There are moments in life when we feel overwhelmed because of the trials and challenges in our path. We forget the joy that life brings and instead of seeing the good that surrounds us, we focus more on the bad that is only temporary in nature. In these moments of discouragement it is important that we refocus on the Lord and allow His presence to fill us with the assurance that all will be well. It is easy to come back to the realization that God is in control and our life is secure in His Hands. One only needs to see the beauty that surrounds them. Creation alone should cause us to remember God's omnipotence and His ability to meet the needs of every thing that He has created.

The Bible says that God opens His Hand and satisfies the desire of every living thing. That verse alone should cause us to be thankful that God has not forgotten about us. Our needs are still on His mind. No matter what we go through in life, the Lord will never leave us nor forsake us. He holds us close to His heart and wishes for us to trust Him completely and wholeheartedly. I believe nothing hurts God more than when we doubt His Word. He has established His covenant for a thousand generations, so if God said it, then we can rest in the assurance that it will be done. (Psalm 145:15-19) (1 Chronicles 16:15)

Be encouraged to focus on the blessings before you. Take time to re-strengthen your faith in God's ability. See the beauty that surrounds you. Look at the trees with their leaves that sway so majestically in the cool summer breeze. Smell the magnificent fragrances that overtake your senses when you take a walk on a nice summer day. Listen to the sounds of birds singing their beautiful songs. Their life is free of worry and with their singing they proclaim the majesty of their Creator. See the beauty that the evening and night sky brings with its many changing colors which looks like a masterpiece painted by the hands of The Master. Look at the stars with their glowing luminescence and try to count their number which is infinite to us, but not to God for He calls each one by name. (Psalm 147:4-5)

When we see with refreshed eyes the beauty of God's creation, we will be quicker to trust that our simple needs will be met. The vastness of this world is all being taken care of by the Lord who created it and the Bible says that we are more precious to Him than all of these. So why do we worry? Why do we allow the temporary setbacks to discourage our hearts? It is because we take our eyes off of the Lord who offers perfect peace. We set our eyes on the problem instead of giving thanks and praise to the One who brings all the solutions. (Matthew 6:25-34) (Isaiah 26:3-4)

I encourage you again to see the blessings that surround you. Focus on the good things in your life. Let God know that you are thankful. Send your praises to the Lord and with your whole heart trust God in every area of your life. When you do, your anxiety will be replaced with peace and the trials that first brought discouragement will be replaced with a deep knowing that All Is Well.

Being At Peace In The Midst of Adversity

It is important that we focus on the right things when discouragement tries to infiltrate our being. We must have our minds set on things above and not on things below. We should never allow a temporary setback to make us murmur and complain about how tough things are, but rather we should use that situation to remind us of the goodness of God, of the many times that He has delivered us in times past and made us better because of them. The lessons that are learned through the trials are priceless. No matter how bad a situation may seem in that moment, it is serving a purpose even if we don't realize it in that moment. What we must do is stay in peace, trust that God is in control and have a deep and assured knowing that all will be well in the end. I know the benefits of staying at peace in the midst of difficulty firsthand. Ever since I gave my life to the Lord, I have been at peace in Him. I've had a childlike trust that God is with me and that nothing shall be able to take me out of His Hands. (Colossians 3:1-2) (Romans 5:3-5) (James 1:2-4)

Recently, I had a minor health scare. I had been having some issues with my stomach and no medicine was really helping. I tried antibiotics and that didn't solve the problem. I finally went to my doctor and had an x-ray done to see if they could find anything wrong internally. A couple days later my doctor called and wanted me to have a CT Scan because they found a "mass" near my pelvis.

When we hear that word mass, it makes one think of cancer, but I chose not to believe that. I was very calm and at peace and knew that nothing would come my way that God didn't already have the provision for. It took nine days to schedule the scan and another day to get the results back, but when we did I was not really surprised.

In those nine days that I was waiting to get the scan, I was not worried, I was not fearful, I was not complaining, I was acting as I normally did. Nothing in my demeanor changed. I stayed focused on the goodness of God and I knew that all things would work together for my good. When I next saw the doctor to get the results, he was amazed that there was nothing there. That mass that was visible on the x-ray had disappeared and after taking a different set of antibiotics, my stomach issue was resolved. (Romans 8:28)

The reason I'm sharing this is because I want you to have that same trust and assurance that all will be well no matter what the report says and no matter how bleak the situation may seem right now. Stay in peace no matter how hard the storms are raging and no matter how tempted you are to murmur and complain. If the Lord hasn't left you in times past, then why would He leave you now? In those times of uncertainty, I would encourage you to bless the Lord with your words of praise and thanksgiving. Let your confession be praise filled. Speak only positive, overcoming and authoritative words of victory over your situation. Don't murmur, don't complain and don't magnify the negatives, but rather magnify all of the positives. Remember your past victories and make every effort to focus on the right things. When you do, you will see your situation turn around to bless you and make you better than you were before it. (Hebrews 13:5-6) (Philippians 2:14-15)

Praise the Lord who is good, whose mercies are renewed every day and whose love never decreases towards us.

It Is A Beautiful Day Today

It is a beautiful day today! Do you agree? I hope so. Depending on when you are reading this, it may be sunny, raining or snowing outside, but that does not change the fact that it's a beautiful day. It's a beautiful day not because of the season or because of the weather, it is beautiful because we are able to see it, enjoy it and get from it the beauty that it offers. Every day is beautiful and with each new day that we are lucky enough to have, we receive with it a new chance and a new opportunity to live life to the fullest and recognize how lucky we are to have this day.

Many times we get sidetracked with the busyness of life and we rush through our days as if we are in a race and we don't take the time to enjoy the blessings that surround us. We shouldn't wait for life to get less hectic to start enjoying our days, but rather we should realize that tomorrow is not promised to us and we shouldn't postpone for tomorrow what could be had today. Today we can spend time with our family and friends. Today we can slow down to smell the flowers, to watch the sunset, to stare up at the stars and appreciate the beauty that each one offers. (Psalm 118:24) (James 4:13-15)

So many times we look at the calendar and wonder where the days went. We're amazed at how fast years go by and without realizing it then, we see how much we have missed. We regret not taking the opportunities that we had to live life to the full because we were so busy. We must remember to make time to enjoy the simple things. We are to make a conscious decision to not repeat the past where we did not take advantage to enjoy the day in the simplest of ways. Life will always be busy, we will always have something that needs to be done, but if we don't stop and look around and appreciate this day, they will all pass by in a blur and we will be filled with regrets not because we let one year pass us by, but because a lifetime was spent hurrying and we didn't take time to slow down and smell the roses. (Nehemiah 8:10)

I encourage you to think about how you are spending your days. Are you rushing through them? Are they all a blur in your memory? If so, then you need to reevaluate what's most important and make a conscious decision to start enjoying this beautiful day. It is a beautiful day. Make the most of it :)

<u>You Are Not Alone</u>

No matter the trials, tribulations and setbacks of life, we should always remember that we are not alone in this world. Challenges may come our way, but we don't have to face them alone. We have the support of family and friends who are there to lift us up when we can't stand on our own. We have the love of those closest to us who will be there for us no matter what comes our way. Sometimes we just need to be reminded that we are not alone in this world. When we face difficulties, many times we want to face them alone because we believe the lie that nobody cares about our well-being. The truth is people care more than we can possibly think or imagine, we just have to allow them to come in and help us overcome our challenges. (Galatians 6:2)

Overcoming challenges on our own will never be as easy as overcoming them with someone by our side. Receiving encouragement, inspiration, and hope from those closest to us helps us to believe in ourselves again and motivates us to face our challenges with a renewed vigor and an unwavering resolve that we will overcome and be triumphant over every obstacle in our path. The support that we receive strengthens us from the inside out because we are shown that we are loved and cared about. When these two simple affirmations are received, our determination to overcome becomes multiplied many times over. (Ecclesiastes 4:9-12)

Be encouraged to receive the support that you need to overcome the trials in your path. Don't think of facing your obstacles alone because you will find the road that is traveled alone much more difficult than when it is traveled with the support, love and encouragement that comes with those whom we love the most. We can think back on our past trials and see that it was the blessing of having someone else with us that made overcoming that trial that much easier. Always welcome help when you need it. Don't face your challenges alone because thinking that you can do it on your own may bring discouragement, depression and even failure. (1 Thessalonians 5:11-15) (Acts 20:35)

The Bible emphasizes our need for help as we read in Ecclesiastes 4:9-10 "Two people are better than one, because they get more done by working together. If one falls down, the other can help him up. But it is bad for the person who is alone and falls, because no one is there to help." I encourage you again to receive help when you need it. Don't allow pride, arrogance or ego to keep you from reaching the heights of victory that God has for you.

God's Strength And Our Weakness

The Lord has spoken to my heart to write a message on His strength and our weakness and how we can be used greatly by God when we acknowledge and recognize that when we are at our weakest, it is then that we are at our strongest in Him. If you are feeling discouraged in your faith, I hope that you will be lifted up and inspired through this message that will show you the power of God's strength and ability when we are at our weakest in strength and spirit.

The Lord declares in 2 Corinthians 12:9, "...for My strength is made perfect in weakness." There are many moments in life that we think we are unable to do God's work because of some weakness or undeveloped ability. We need to keep in mind and remember that God loves to work through those that are humble in spirit and ready to obey His voice in any circumstance. God's power cannot be manifested through our life when we are proud and arrogant, but when we are humble before the Lord and acknowledge our weakness, it is then that God's strength manifests itself through our life. (1 Peter 5:5-7)

Concerning God's strength when we are at our weakest, I think of the Apostle Paul. There was a time when Paul was greatly bothered by a thorn that the enemy placed on his side. Paul prayed three different times and asked God to take this thorn from his side, but God replied and said to him, "My grace is sufficient unto thee." The Apostle Paul was strengthened by God's word and then went on to say that great verse of scripture that gives me strength when I am weak. Paul says, "...for when I am weak, then am I strong." Take encouragement in the Lord and know that your weakness is not a negative in the eyes of the Lord, but an opportunity to show His strength through your life. (2 Corinthians 12:9-10) (Philippians 4:13)

We need to remember that most of the people God used throughout the Bible were people that were not qualified for their positions. Moses couldn't speak well and yet through God's strength and direction, Moses led the Children of Israel out of slavery in Egypt and directed them to their promised land. David was a young shepherd boy and yet through God's power, he killed the giant warrior Goliath with just one stone of his slingshot. David went on to be a king and was greatly used by the Lord throughout his life. The Apostle Paul before his conversion was the chief oppressor of the Christians. God called him to serve, changed his name and used him to preach the gospel of Jesus Christ. Because of his obedience, Paul is regarded as one of the greatest Apostle's and a man who changed the world for Jesus Christ. (Exodus 4:10-12) (1 Samuel 17:14-54) (Acts 9:1-22)

God's ways are not our ways and so when God chooses His servants, He does not always choose the able, but the unable because the able may be tempted to accept the glory for their work, whereas the unable know that God did it all and He alone deserves the Glory for His work. If God wanted strength, He could command His angels to do what He asks. We need to remember that in the Old

Testament, one Angel killed 185,000 people that were planning to attack the city of Jerusalem. God is not impressed by strength, but He is impressed by weakness and humility and a heart that seeks after Him. (Isaiah 55:8-9) (Isaiah 37:33-36) (2 Corinthians 12:6) (Isaiah 6:8)

And so I encourage you today if you are seeking God to be used of Him to come to God with a humble heart and ask the Lord to use you for His glory. Never allow pride or weakness to keep you from fulfilling God's plan for your life. God will do great things with us when we simply acknowledge that it is not in our strength that we are successful, but it is only in the strength of the Lord. (Jeremiah 29:12) (Zechariah 4:6)

So, you say "You are weak in your abilities", that's great because in God's eyes that is when you are the strongest.

Read and meditate on these scriptures:

2 Corinthians 12:8-10 "For this thing I besought the Lord thrice, that it might depart from me. And He said unto me, My grace is sufficient for thee: for My strength is made perfect in weakness. Most gladly therefore will I rather glory in my infirmities, that the power of Christ may rest upon me. Therefore I take pleasure in infirmities, in reproaches, in necessities, in persecutions, in distresses for Christ's sake: for when I am weak, then am I strong."

1 Peter 5:5-7 "Likewise, ye younger, submit yourselves unto the elder. Yea, all of you be subject one to another,

and be clothed with humility: for God resisteth the proud, and giveth grace to the humble. Humble yourselves therefore under the mighty hand of God, that He may exalt you in due time: Casting all your care upon Him; for He careth for you."

1 Samuel 16:7 "But the LORD said unto Samuel, Look not on his countenance, or on the height of his stature; because I have refused him: for the LORD seeth not as man seeth; for man looketh on the outward appearance, but the LORD looketh on the heart."

Psalm 30:10-12 "Hear, O LORD, and have mercy upon me: LORD, be thou my helper. Thou hast turned for me my mourning into dancing: Thou hast put off my sackcloth, and girded me with gladness; To the end that my glory may sing praise to Thee, and not be silent. O LORD my God, I will give thanks unto Thee for ever."

All scriptures can be found in the King James Version Bible.

No Man Is Beyond God's Redemption

There are many people in this world who doubt the supremacy of the Lord Jesus Christ. They think of Jesus Christ as a prophet, a teacher, a wise man, but in no way was He the Son of God who came to earth to die for the sins of the world and redeem mankind from their unrighteousness. They don't trust that Jesus is who He says He is and instead of surrendering their life to the Lord, they foolishly go the other way trusting more in their own intellect rather than in the One who created them. It is my hope that this message on trusting in the Lord Jesus Christ will turn some of those who have forsaken the Lord to come back and be reconciled with Him.

There is no greater testimony of redemption and reconciliation than that of the Apostle Paul. The testimony of the Apostle Paul should give every person the proof they need to know that Jesus Christ is the Son of God, that He has all power in Heaven and on Earth and that it is only through Jesus Christ that we can be saved, redeemed and reconciled back to God again. The story of the Apostle Paul is one that is encouraging, inspiring, motivating and most importantly it is proof positive that the Lord Jesus Christ is forgiving even to the worst sinner and He can use them in ways that they never thought or imagined. (John 3:16-17) (Matthew 28:18-19) (Isaiah 1:18)

The Apostle Paul was born named Saul or more commonly known as Saul of Tarsus. He was a Jew by birth and he was a scholar in all of the Jewish laws and practices. There was nothing in the Jewish law that he was not masterful of since his youth. When the Lord Jesus Christ's name became more and more prominent, it was Saul's mission to destroy Christianity and to punish and or kill all those who preached the name of the Lord Jesus Christ. Saul felt he was doing God's work when he was killing those "false prophets" who were preaching that Christ had risen from the dead, that He was alive and that He had power to save and redeem mankind from their sins. (Acts 26:4-5) (Acts 26:9-11)

When Saul of Tarsus was given the task to seek those who were preaching Christ and bring them to Jerusalem for judgment, he took the job proudly feeling he was justified in bringing to justice those who were falsely preaching God's Word. It was on that journey towards Damascus when Saul's plans to destroy Christianity were suddenly and eternally reversed. On his way to bring persecution to the Christians, the Lord Jesus Christ appeared in the sky and asked Saul a simple question that forever changed his destiny. The Lord Jesus asked "Saul, Saul, why are you persecuting Me?" Saul did not know who he was speaking to and asked who are you and the Lord answered and said "I am Jesus whom you are persecuting." The Lord then gave Saul instructions on what to do next and he followed what the Lord told him and that was the beginning of the transformation from Saul the persecutor into Paul the preacher. (Acts 9:3-6)

Now called Paul, he took his new mission to preach Christ with the same zeal and fervor that he had before, but now he knew what his real purpose was. He was to use his life to tell everyone that Jesus Christ is the Son of God and that it is only through Him that we can be forgiven and redeemed from every sin and every shortfall. He preached that a new beginning is available to anyone who calls upon the name of the Lord. The Apostle Paul once being the chief persecutor of Christians was now the chief advocate for Christ. God's power came upon Paul in marvelous ways. He preached with conviction, he healed those who were afflicted and he used his testimony of persecution against the Christians prior to his conversion to show that God's love is beyond our comprehension and that His forgiveness is without limit. The man who was once determined to drive people away from Christ now had a stronger conviction to lead people to Christ to be saved and redeemed. (Acts 9:20-22) (Acts 26:20-23) (1 Timothy 1:12-17)

God used the Apostle Paul in wonderful ways. His preaching helped to bring countless souls into God's kingdom. Paul's writings take up half of the New Testament. He encouraged, he challenged, he inspired, he edified, he affirmed and he showed us that even the worst sinner is not beyond redemption. He showed through his life and testimony that a new beginning is always available with God. God's forgiveness towards us is beyond our comprehension. Even when we do wrong, we are not beyond God's mercy and grace. We can be reconciled; we can be forgiven, redeemed and made new again just as the Apostle Paul was. (Acts 9:26-28)

God used a man to bring glory and honor to His Name that no one else thought would be possible. Even the Christians who learned of Paul's conversion were skeptical because of his infamous past, but that is the great thing about God; He doesn't see us for who we were, but rather He sees us for who we can be in Him. Remember what Isaiah 55:8-9 declares "For My thoughts are not your thoughts, neither are your ways My ways, saith the LORD. For as the heavens are higher than the earth, so are My ways higher than your ways, and My thoughts than your thoughts."

Be encouraged to see for yourself through the testimony of Paul that Jesus Christ is alive, that He is the Son of God and that He has all power in heaven and on earth. All who come to The Lord Jesus will be renewed and refreshed. There is no want in them that trust Him. Call upon the Lord and be reconciled. The Lord will forgive and make new every soul that calls upon His Name. He will not cast you away, but He will make you a new creation with new dreams and new possibilities. We have nothing to lose and all to gain with Jesus Christ. I pray that you will receive Him for yourself today if you have not already made that eternal decision.

Read and meditate on these scriptures:

Isaiah 55:6-7 "Seek ye the LORD while He may be found, call ye upon Him while He is near: Let the wicked forsake his way, and the unrighteous man his thoughts: and let him return unto the LORD, and He will have mercy upon him; and to our God, for He will abundantly pardon."

John 3:16-17 Jesus declares "For God so loved the world, that He gave His only begotten Son, that whosoever believeth in Him should not perish, but have everlasting life. For God sent not His Son into the world to condemn the world; but that the world through Him might be saved."

1 Corinthians 2:9-10 "...Eye hath not seen, nor ear heard, neither have entered into the heart of man, the things which God hath prepared for them that love Him. But God hath revealed them unto us by His Spirit: for the Spirit searcheth all things, yea, the deep things of God."

1 Peter 2:9-10 "But ye are a chosen generation, a royal priesthood, an Holy nation, a peculiar people; that ye should shew forth the praises of Him who hath called you out of darkness into His marvellous light: Which in time past were not a people, but are now the people of God: which had not obtained mercy, but now have obtained mercy."

Deuteronomy 4:30-31 "When thou art in tribulation, and all these things are come upon thee, even in the latter days, if thou turn to the LORD thy God, and shalt be obedient unto His voice; (For the LORD thy God is a merciful God;) He will not forsake thee, neither destroy thee, nor forget the covenant of thy fathers which He sware unto them."

Revelation 3:20 Jesus declares "Behold, I stand at the door, and knock: if any man hear My voice, and open the door, I will come in to him, and will sup with him, and he with Me."

All of these scriptures can be found in the King James Version Bible.

Focusing On The Good In Our Lives

It is easy to get down, discouraged and even depressed when we look at a negative situation and can't see any good coming from it. What we must remember is that life is all about overcoming the challenges that come our way. We can murmur and complain that our situation is so tough or we can gird ourselves up and dig our heels in with determination that we will come out of this situation better than we were before it. Our attitude will dictate the outcome of our situation. We can yell at the darkness and complain about how dark it is or we can light a match and illuminate that situation. We must train ourselves to look on the bright side no matter what we face in life. If it is a financial hardship, a health crisis, a family situation or a personal trial that we are facing, we have to tell ourselves that we are still blessed, favored and chosen by the Lord to be triumphant in the end. We must enthuse ourselves in the difficult times. We must remember where we were in times past and what we've overcome throughout our life. (James 1:12)

Remembering our triumphs encourages us in the difficult times. When we recall what we've overcome, we become encouraged to face the trials with a renewed determination and a renewed vigor. Be encouraged to look on the bright side, see the good that is still enveloping your life and make an extra effort to let God know that you are thankful that He is with you and that your eyes of faith are focused on Him and not on your situation. A simple quote I think upon often says "Don't tell God how big your problems are, but rather tell your problems how big your God is." I encourage you again to focus on the good that is before you. See how fortunate you are. Think upon your blessings and you will find your problems shrink by comparison. (Psalm 34:1-4)

Being At Peace At All Times

We should always have a lighthearted attitude and not allow ourselves to take life so seriously. Many times we allow the temporary trials and setbacks of life to ruin our days and make us lose our joy and peace. What we must remember and keep in mind is that it is in our hands how we react to a situation. We can either act in faith or we can act in fear. We can have a demeanor of peace or a demeanor of worry. It is all in how we react to a situation that will ultimately affect its outcome. When we act in a manner of peace and trust that God is in control, that is when all things will work together for our good because we trust God and we are called according to His purposes. (Psalm 68:3-6) (Romans 8:28)

Whenever you feel tempted to lose your peace, remind yourself of the greatness of God. Think of the many times that He intervened in times past and delivered you from a tough situation. Remember your many blessings that God has graciously given to you and know that it is God who wishes for you to be at peace and rest in Him. The Lord Jesus Christ conquered death and hell on our behalf so that we can rest in His finished work. There is no need for us to worry about anything. The Lord is in control of all things, even our very breath. He is omniscient, omnipotent and omnipresent. The Lord knows all things at all times in all places. There is nothing that can surprise God and there is no problem that God can't help us to overcome. (Isaiah 26:3-4) (Psalm 61:1-5)

Always remember that God is our protector, our comforter, our guide, our inspiration, our leader and our King. Let us have a countenance of peace no matter what comes our way and bring into remembrance the greatness of our God. He is all things and in Him lies every answer to our every desire. Trust Him, depend on Him and let God know that your eyes of faith are focused on the Great I AM no matter what comes your way.

A Lesson From The Titanic

I was listening to a minister recently and he was speaking on the most important thing a person can do in their lifetime. His message of course was on accepting the free gift of Salvation through the shed blood of Jesus Christ. I began thinking about how true this is since in life we never know when our time on earth will end.

I began thinking about the story and tragic ending of the Titanic, which is the ship that was deemed unsinkable, yet after 4 days into her maiden voyage, the unsinkable ship hit an iceberg and sank in less than 3 hours. This happened on April 15th, 1912 and up until that date, the ship was considered the greatest achievement ever created by the hand of man. It took over 15,000 men to build the ship and more than 3 years to complete.

The maiden voyage lured the "very best people:" British nobility, American industrialists, the very cream of New York and Philadelphia society. It also attracted many poor emigrants, hoping to start a new life in America or Canada. It was recorded as the most luxurious ship ever built and had some of the most important people of that time on board.

On April 14, 1912, only 3 days after leaving Southampton England on her way to the United States, the Titanic hit an iceberg on the starboard side which caused a series of gashes below the waterline in the storage compartments, which filled with water and eventually caused the ship to sink. In the end, there were only 705 survivors out of the 2228 that boarded only days earlier.

When the news of the Titanic's sinking reached town, people only wanted to know one thing; how many people were rescued and how many people were lost. It did not matter about their possessions or net worth or how many letters of achievement they had after their name. The only thing that mattered was; how many were "saved" and how many were "lost".

This is the point I wanted to make about this message. When our life on earth is said and done, it will not matter how much money we have in our bank account or the number of accomplishments we achieved. The only thing that matters when we stand before God is; are we saved because of our belief and confession in the Lord Jesus Christ, or are we lost because we never made time to make Jesus the Lord of our life.

Only through Jesus Christ can we make it to heaven, for the Bible declares in Acts 4:12 "Nor is there salvation in any other, for there is no other name under heaven given among men by which we must be saved". We cannot go to heaven because we do good things or because we are good people because if this were the case then Christ died in vain. (Galatians 2:21)

Our good works cannot save us for the Bible declares in Isaiah 64:6 "But we are all like an unclean thing, and all our righteousness are like filthy rags..." We could never measure up to God's standards, but the good news is; Jesus came to earth and willfully gave His life for you and I and all we need to do is trust in Him and the work that He completed on the cross for all mankind. (John 19:30)

I encourage you to make Jesus the Lord of your life if you haven't already. There is no difference in color or nationality. Jesus is able to save and deliver all who call upon His name. I want you to know there is Joy in heaven because of one sinner that repents and the angel's of God rejoice over that soul that has been saved, so never think God does not care about you or that you are so bad that God will not forgive you. He will forgive each of us, but we must ask for His forgiveness. (Luke 15:10) (Romans 10:12-13)

Just as the Titanic was deemed unsinkable and was promised to be afloat forever, many people go through life thinking there is time to get right with God and serve the Lord after all the fun has been fulfilled, but that is a trick of the enemy. He will do anything to try to postpone your decision for Christ, so be alert of his evil devices and know that today is the accepted time for salvation as the Bible declares in 2 Corinthians 6:2 "...Behold, now is the accepted time; behold, now is the day of salvation."

Read and meditate on these scriptures and know that God will forgive you and receive you unto Himself:

Ezekiel 33:11 "Say to them: 'As I live,' says the Lord GOD, 'I have no pleasure in the death of the wicked, but that the wicked turn from his way and live. Turn, turn from your evil ways! For why should you die...?'"

1 John 1:9-10 "If we confess our sins, He is faithful and just to forgive us our sins and to cleanse us from all unrighteousness. If we say that we have not sinned, we make Him a liar, and His word is not in us."

Isaiah 55:6-7 "Seek the LORD while He may be found, Call upon Him while He is near. Let the wicked forsake his way, And the unrighteous man his thoughts; Let him return to the LORD, And He will have mercy on him; And to our God, For He will abundantly pardon."

Romans 10:9-10 "...If you confess with your mouth the Lord Jesus and believe in your heart that God has raised Him from the dead, you will be saved. For with the heart one believes unto righteousness, and with the mouth confession is made unto salvation."

1 John 5:11-13 "And this is the testimony: that God has given us eternal life, and this life is in His Son. He who has the Son has life; he who does not have the Son of God does not have life. These things I have written to you who believe in the name of the Son of God, that you may know that you have eternal life, and that you may continue to believe in the name of the Son of God."

All scriptures can be found in the New King James Version.

Recognizing Our Many Blessings

There are moments in life when we get down on ourselves because we focus on what we don't have and we find ourselves becoming discouraged not realizing that our blessings and God's favor upon our life are not being recognized by us. We sometimes become so focused at what we are missing that we neglect to see all that we possess. When we take the time to reflect on the abundance that we have been fortunate enough to have, that is when our ungratefulness for our many blessings will begin to cease. It is in looking at what we do have that will make our hearts overflow with joy and gratitude. (Psalm 103:1-8) (Psalm 18:46-49)

Seeing the love of our family and friends, being thankful for our health, appreciating our jobs, taking the time to enjoy and reflect on the beauty of life that surrounds us are very simple ways to see how fortunate we really are. Be encouraged to change your focus and see the blessings that you possess if you're finding yourself quickly forgetting how much you have to be thankful for. When we take the time to count our blessings, we will quickly lose count of the things that were so prominent in our minds before.

Letting God Lead Our Life

The goodness and mercy of the Lord reach beyond even the greatest borders. The Lord wishes to direct each of our lives on to the best path possible, but we must be sensitive to follow His direction at all times. It is in our prayer time that we are most available in being receptive to the direction of the Lord. We cannot expect the Lord to be quick in leading our life when we are lackadaisical in our prayers and not committed in following the still small voice of the Holy Spirit. (Isaiah 30:21)

We are to be steadfast and continuous in our prayer life both so we can be sensitive to His direction as well as to receive the spiritual strength that each of us need to continue on. Be encouraged to pray and seek the Lord's direction for your life because it is God's will for you to prosper and be in good health even as your soul prospers. (1 Kings 19:11-12) (3 John 2)

Focusing On The Good Before Us

With the many pressures and stresses of daily life, it is important that we have a lighthearted attitude and see the good that is before us. It is easy for anyone to murmur and complain about all their hardships, but we who have given our life to the Lord should remember His peace that surpasses all understanding. The Lord promises to keep us in perfect peace because our mind is stayed on Him. There is no need for us to worry or stress about our future. The Lord holds our future securely in the palms of His Hands. If God tells us not to worry about anything, then we should believe Him. We should take God at His Word. What will we gain by complaining? What will we benefit by worrying? I have tried both in times past and realized my situation didn't improve a bit, in fact it got worse. When we give a negative situation more attention, we are in essence expanding or increasing it, but when we realize that God is in control of all things, then we will be more at ease and we will see that situation be resolved in ways that we had never even thought of. (Philippians 4:6-7) (Isaiah 26:3)

Be encouraged to laugh more, enjoy the blessings that surround you and be quick to be thankful for all that God has given you. An attitude of praise will brighten our life and our future. When we recognize God's goodness and we are quick to thank Him and show our appreciation, God will be pleased and will reward us in like manner. A thankful heart will be a blessed heart. An appreciative spirit will be a filled spirit. Don't give a negative situation more of your energy, but rather use that energy in a positive manner to pray, praise and give thanks to the Lord above who will bring every answer that your heart seeks. The Bible tells us to pray in faith believing and because we do, we will receive the answer. (Psalm 34:1-10) (Psalm 139:14-18)

I encourage you again to smile more, enjoy life while you are living and use every opportunity that comes before you to show your faithfulness to the Lord. He is the one who will deliver us and who deserves the most attention from His people. (James 5:13-15)

Becoming Stronger Through Our Trials

Many times we feel life is overwhelming when all we see is trials, struggles and setbacks. What we must realize is that we have an opportunity with each trial that comes before us. We can use that struggle to our benefit by recognizing that in our power we can accomplish nothing, but when we trust and depend on the Lord, that is when mountains can move. When we stay in peace despite the hardships, despite the heartaches, despite the troubles, that is when miracles can happen. I have learned that the darkest of days is followed by the brightest of sunshine's. When I have faced my greatest challenge that is when my greatest victory followed. What we must remember is that our character is strengthened by friction. It is strengthened by going through the fire. It is strengthened by overcoming the obstacles before us. Just as muscle grows by first being torn down, so it is with us. By going through the tough times our faith becomes stronger, our will becomes resilient, our hearts become unwavering and our trust in God becomes never ending. (John 15:5) (Job 23:10)

Be encouraged to see with your eyes of faith the end result of the path that you are still traveling on. See that you will overcome every trial before you. See that you will be strong because of the obstacles that were in your path. See that your faith will be unyielding because you didn't give up. Knowing that God is still by our side helping us fight each battle encourages our hearts to know the storms of life are not here to stay, but they will soon pass. Just as it is darkest before the dawn, so will our sorrow turn into the greatest joy. When we focus on the end result, we will not be discouraged by the struggles we currently are going through. We will have known the secret to peace that surpasses all understanding. Peace comes in knowing that our life is securely in the Hands of the Lord and nothing can take us away from Him. Rejoice in the midst of your difficulty. Give God thanks that your answer is on the way and have a deep knowing that in God's sight All Is Well! (Hebrews 11:1) (Philippians 3:13-14) (Psalm 138:7-8)

Blessing Our Today's To The Fullest

There are many people in this world who fear what tomorrow holds. Instead of enjoying and relishing in today, they go through their today's worried about their tomorrow's. What they fail to realize is that tomorrow is promised to no man. We have today to live, laugh and be merry. Whether we choose to do so however is completely up to us. We can either use this day to bring happiness to ourselves and to others or we can wallow in self pity and self doubt. What we must realize is that this is a blessed day. It is beautiful, bright and ready to be taken a hold of. Today's possibilities are only limited by our imagination. We can share joy with it, we can share laughter with it, we can bring encouragement, inspiration, and blessings with it if we choose to see the beauty that today offers us. (James 4:13-15) (Psalm 31:7-8)

No matter what you may be going through and no matter the obstacles that are in your path, I encourage you to enjoy today to the best of your ability. See the beauty that surrounds you by going for a walk in the park, take in the refreshing smell of a freshly cut flower, play with your pet, laugh with your child, eat some ice cream, do something that will bring a smile to your face and joy to your spirit. Change your mentality and focus on the good before you. Give thanks to God for every blessing that He has graciously given to you and with your whole heart see how fortunate you really are. Doing something that changes the monotony of your normal routine will positively affect your mindset and give you something new to focus on. (Psalm 34:1-4)

Make it a daily challenge to focus on something good before you and be thankful for it. Be determined to enjoy today no matter how tempted you are to worry or fear what tomorrow holds. By doing so, you will be blessing your days and starving your doubts. Remember what Psalm 118:24 declares "This is the day the Lord has made, we will rejoice and be glad in it."

Using Our Experiences To Our Benefit

We should always remember to take time and learn the lessons of life. Everything we go through whether good or bad will serve a purpose for us down the road. Either we'll have great memories that we can think on when the storms of life are raging or we can use the bad experiences to learn lessons so that our future will be made better because of them. It is within our ability how we see our days. Every experience can be used to our benefit to strengthen our spirit and our resolve. Never see the bad experiences as time wasted because in most cases the tough times strengthened our backbone and shows us how strong we really are. When we recognize that we are made better, stronger and wiser by the tough times, that is when we can go through them with a quiet confidence that this tough time is serving a purpose to make us even more resilient than we were before. (2 Corinthians 12:8-10) (2 Corinthians 4:16-18)

Never allow yourself to get down, discouraged or question your life's purpose. See this day as an opportunity to use all of your past experience to make the best of where you are right now. Use the wisdom that you've attained to change your mindset. See the negatives and change them into positives. If you've lost your job, see it as an opportunity to excel in a better position. If your health isn't at its best, use what you learned from what you've done wrong in times past and make better decisions now to improve your health by eating better, exercising more and simply treating your body with respect realizing that it is the temple of the Holy Spirit. (1 Corinthians 6:19-20)

No matter what experiences we've had, we can use them to better our situation right now. We don't have to look at the glass as half empty, but we can see it as more than half-full and on its way to overflowing. It's not a matter of positive thinking, but rather it is a life choice to bless our life with our words, our deeds and our actions. Be encouraged to do all that you can to use every experience to your advantage. Whether it was good or bad, use it to your benefit. All that you have learned and attained from your years of living, use it to your advantage to better your life right now. When you do, you will be proud of how you've used your past experiences and made them work for you in this present time and in your future to come.

Having Faith And Confidence In God

It is easy for anyone to want to give up when all they see are obstacles in their path. What we must realize as we travel through this journey called life is that God never promised that we would be trouble-free and live life on flowery beds of ease. In fact, the Lord Jesus knew that life is full of troubles and wanted to comfort His Saints by saying in John 16:33 "These things I have spoken unto you, that in Me ye might have peace. In the world ye shall have tribulation: but be of good cheer; I have overcome the world." We are to put on the countenance of peace and have faith in God that all will work out for our good in the end. Faith must be shown with action behind it. We can't say we trust God one moment and then murmur and complain about all the wrong that was going on in our life the next moment. We must be steadfast and unmoved by what we see with our physical eyes and know that God is still with us and has not left our side. (Proverbs 15:13) (Romans 8:28)

No matter what is going wrong in your life, I want you to know that God is still in control. No matter the illness, the financial issue or family trouble, I encourage you to stay in faith. Let God know that your eyes are not focused on the problem, but they are focused on Him. Speak to God in prayer. Confess all that is on your heart. The Lord knows you better than you know yourself and when we acknowledge our frailty and confess our need for God; that is when heaven and earth will move on your behalf. We may not get the answers in ways that we expect, but God is faithful to bring peace to our hearts and comfort us in our trials to let us know that all is well. I know I've asked God for relief many times and He always answered my prayer. It may not have been immediate, but it was never too late. Trust the Lord, be confident in His ability to restore peace in your heart and know that no matter what happens, your life will always be secure in His Hands. (Psalm 103:8-14) (Isaiah 55:6-9) (Hebrews 13:5-7)

Trusting In Jesus

We should never be too hard on ourselves when we fall short and fail to meet God's standard for righteousness. We must remember that we are all imperfect and flawed human beings who are in need of God's grace and mercy to carry us through our days. The Lord is righteous in all His ways and perfect in all His acts and knowing our need for salvation, He sent His only begotten Son to the earth to take upon Himself our sins and died in our stead. Never believe the lie that God does not love you. His love is so great for mankind that He willingly took our sins so that in the fullness of time we might be made righteous in the eyes of God Almighty. (Psalm 116:4-9) (John 3:16)

The gift that was given to us is undeserved, but still is available to all who acknowledge their sin, repent and open their hearts to the Lord Jesus Christ. There is no other way to God or heaven, except through the finished work of the Lord Jesus Christ. Call upon Him today giving Jesus all of your heartbreak, shortfalls, burdens, disappointments and allow Him to replace them with His Peace, Joy and Love that surpasses all understanding. (Romans 10:9-13) (Luke 15:4-7) (Acts 4:12)

Having Peace In The Midst Of Our Difficulty

Many times we feel life is overwhelming when all we see is trials, struggles and setbacks. What we must realize is that we have an opportunity with each trial that comes before us. We can use that struggle to our benefit by recognizing that in our power we can accomplish nothing, but when we trust and depend on the Lord, that is when mountains can move. When we stay in peace despite the hardships, despite the heartaches, despite the troubles, that is when miracles can happen. I have learned that the darkest of days is followed by the brightest of sunshine's. When I have faced my greatest challenge that is when my greatest victory followed. What we must remember is that our character is strengthened by friction. It is strengthened by going through the fire. It is strengthened by overcoming the obstacles before us. Just as muscle grows by first being torn down, so it is with us. By going through the tough times our faith becomes stronger, our will becomes resilient, our hearts become unwavering and our trust in God becomes never ending. (John 15:5) (Philippians 4:13) (Matthew 17:20)

Be encouraged to see with your eyes of faith the end result of the path that you are still traveling on. See that you will overcome every trial before you. See that you will be strong because of the obstacles that were in your path. See that your faith will be unyielding because you didn't give up. Knowing that God is still by our side helping us fight each battle encourages our hearts to know the storms of life are not here to stay, but they will soon pass. Just as it is darkest before the dawn, so will our sorrow turn into the greatest joy. When we focus on the end result, we will not be discouraged by the struggles we are currently going through. We will have known the secret to peace that surpasses all understanding. Peace comes in knowing that our life is securely in the Hands of the Lord and nothing can take us away from Him. Rejoice in the midst of your difficulty. Give God thanks that's your answer is on the way and have a deep knowing that in God's sight All Is Well! (2 Kings 6:15-17) (Philippians 4:6-7) (John 14:27)

Continuing To Believe In Ourselves

We should never give up in believing that we are meant to accomplish great things with our life. There are moments when we fail at a certain task and we believe the lie that we're not good enough or that our best days are behind us. What we must remember is that falling down is a part of life. We must accept that not every trial will be a success and that failing doesn't mean that we have failed; it simply means that we have another opportunity to try again to reach success. Some of the greatest inventors the world has ever known saw nothing but failure over and over and over again, but they didn't give up. They knew they were meant for more. They knew that greatness was within their reach. They just had to get through the failing stage until victory and success was within their grasp. (Psalm 37:23-25) (Psalm 145:14-19)

Our greatest challenge is staying encouraged in the midst of the struggle, in the midst of the difficulty, in the midst of the failing stage and realize that success will come if we don't give in or give up. We are to be confident in the dreams and abilities that God has placed within our hearts and be steadfast in our faith that no matter what challenge we face, victory will be ours. No matter what is going on around us and no matter what everyone else is doing, let us hold on to our dreams and be determined to bring them to pass. The Bible declares in Ephesians 6:13-14 "Wherefore take unto you the whole armour of God, that ye may be able to withstand in the evil day, and having done all, to stand. Stand therefore..." We are to hold fast on what we know is our mission and do all that we can to bring it to pass. (Psalm 112:1-7) (1 Peter 5:5-7) (Psalm 37:3-8)

Whatever goals you have in your heart, hold on to them and don't let go. Whether it is a calling from God to do His work or a more personal goal that has been resonating in your heart, you should never believe that you can't accomplish it. Believe in yourself as God believes in you and be diligent in your pursuit. Don't give in to negativity, discouragement or the naysayers. Believe, dream, dare and stay faithful until you reach the success that you have aimed for. It may seem impossible in the beginning, but stay faithful until impossible becomes reality. (Ephesians 6:10) (Proverbs 8:13-19)

Being Thankful For Our Abundance

We each have so much to be thankful for, but many times we allow the temporary trials and setbacks in our life to make us lose focus of our great abundance. What we should do on a daily basis is bring into remembrance all that we have that makes us truly rich so that we can see how blessed and favored we really are. Things that money can't buy such as our family, our children and our health is what should be thought upon when times of discouragement try to bring us down. We should focus on the good things, the happy memories and the things that bring us great joy and then we will find ourselves remembering our blessings and being thankful for them. (Psalm 103:1-5) (Psalm 139:14-18)

No matter what we go through and no matter how difficult our current situation may seem, we still have the ability to give thanks and be appreciative for our life. As deep as the pit may seem right now, we must remember that it's still not the end of the story. Tomorrow a new day will dawn with new promises and new opportunities. We simply must have the proper attitude and be ready for the blessings that are sure coming our way. (Psalm 30:10-12) (Psalm 31:1-5)

Be encouraged to look past your negative situation and think more on the gifts that you've been given. What gifts you say? The gifts of your family, your spouse, your children, your job, your home, your car, your health, your eyes, your ears, your legs, your hands. Think on how difficult life would be without any one of these blessings. When we focus on what we do have, our appreciation for life becomes that much more evident. Remember to give God thanks for your many blessings and with your words, acts and deeds let your life be a living testimony that you are thankful and appreciative for all that you have been given. (Psalm 111:1-5)

<u>Depending On One Another</u>

There are many instances in life when we just want to be left alone. Whether we are going through a breakup, a financial hardship, a health crisis, or just the challenges of life, we think we can handle the situation by ourselves and not need anyone to help us get through. What we must realize is that we are strengthened by the support of our loved ones. They help us to realize that our situation is not the end of the world and with their love they show us that we will overcome the difficult times. What we must realize is that trying times are promised to come to each of us and because they do, we should be quick to help one another through them. Just as we should seek help in our time of need, we should also extend that same help towards those who are going through their own dark hour. Supporting one another, loving one another and lifting each other up strengthens both our hearts and our resolve to never give in and never give up. (Hebrews 10:24-25) (Ecclesiastes 4:9-12) (Galatians 6:2-5)

I have learned that it is okay to admit that I don't have all the answers. I know that I can't handle the difficult times all on my own. I see now through experience that allowing others to help carry my burden not only lessens the weight on my shoulders, but it allows those closest to me to feel a sense of satisfaction knowing that they can help make a difficult situation a little bit better. That's what we are on this Earth to do. We are here to love one another, to support one another, to lift one another up and show through our actions; our love, our care and our compassion. Jesus says that on these two commandments lay all of the law. The first is to love God with all of our heart, mind and soul and the second is to love our neighbor as ourselves. Be encouraged to make these two commandments the cornerstone of your life. Love God first and equally to it love your neighbor as you love yourself. By doing so, you are ensuring a blessed life. (John 13:34-35) (John 15:12-17)

Loving Your Life Right Now

It is easy to be appreciative and thankful when we take time to see the abundance of our blessings. When we focus on our family, our children, our health, etc., we will quickly find that our problems don't come close in comparison. It is only when we focus more on what we don't have that we allow discouragement or disappointment to enter into our lives. When we look at someone else's better job, better house, better car, etc., we allow jealousy and envy to enter our hearts and make us forget the many good things that we have to be thankful for. We can't live our life in someone else's shoes and wish to have what they have, but we can live our best life with the many good things that we do possess. We can make the best of our life by focusing more on what we do have rather than on what we seem to be lacking. (2 Corinthians 4:17-18) (Proverbs 23:17-18)

No matter how hard life may get, we can still choose to be thankful. We can bless our life, choose to be happy even in the midst of any difficulty and dare to believe that our latter end will be so much better than our former beginnings. Having the expectancy for good things equips us to face tomorrow with eagerness. Thinking positively about your life will brighten the doorway for your future. Being upbeat, appreciative, thankful, and optimistic is a sure way to bless our days and get us ready to face tomorrow. Be encouraged to bless your life. You do so by being thankful for what you have and being appreciative for all that you've been given. Always remember that you are abundantly blessed and have much to be thankful for. When you don't see it, you just have to focus on the right things and all will be made clear to you. (Psalm 62:5-8) (Matthew 12:36-37)

Knowing That You Have A Purpose

We should always keep in mind that God has a purpose and plan for our life. Even in the times that we don't know what our life's purpose is, we must stay in faith and know that God has created us with special intentions that we are meant to bring to pass and fulfill. We must be steadfast in fulfilling our destiny and never allow the voice of discouragement to take root in our hearts keeping us from becoming all that God wishes for us to become. The Bible says that God knew us before the foundation of the world. He planned our lives even before the Earth was created. Be encouraged and know that you have a special purpose that only you have the ability to bring to pass. (Jeremiah 29:11-13) (Jeremiah 1:5-8) (Ephesians 1:4)

The Lord has instilled within you special ability that no one else possesses. As an original creation, God has given only to you what is necessary to bring to pass all that He has placed within your heart. Never believe the lie that is too late for you. Seek the Lord and ask for His will to be made clear in your life. The Lord will be faithful to hear and answer your heartfelt prayers. (Isaiah 30:21) (Isaiah 55:6)

Holding On To Hope

There are many instances in life when we are tempted to lose our joy and only think about the troubles and problems that are in our path. What we must realize is that it is normal to have problems, it is normal to face difficult circumstances, it is normal to question why a tough situation has come our way. When we realize that we are part of the human race and as such are welcomed into the "problem club", that is when we can face our situation with a renewed outlook seeing that we can come forth victorious in the end even in spite and because of the things that we overcame in times past. God has instilled within each of us unique gifts and talents that no one else possesses. He has given us the fortitude to look a problem head-on and know that we can overcome it. With God on our side, nothing shall be impossible to us. We simply must remember where the power comes from. When we are quick to give God all the credit; that is when miracles take place and supernatural victories overtake us. (John 16:33) (Isaiah 42:8)

No matter what you may be going through, know that you still have the chance to overcome. As long as you have breath in your lungs and hope in your heart, then your story isn't finished yet. You still have the opportunity to come forth better, wiser and stronger than you were before that situation. You must simply dig your heels in the ground and be determined that nothing will be able to hinder what the Lord has promised you. Be encouraged to hold on to hope. Hope is a powerful tool and when used correctly it can help you to believe that you will receive even in the midst of an otherwise impossible looking situation. (Jeremiah 29:11-13) (Psalm 71:5)

When we depend on God and place our hope in Him, then the Lord will move in amazing ways to show Himself strong on behalf of those who put their faith and trust in His abilities. Be encouraged again to hold on to hope. Believe for greater things. Know that tomorrow will be better than today. Don't give up and don't give in. Stay strong and confident because faithful is He who has promised. If God said it, then you can rest assured that it will be done. (2 Chronicles 16:9) (1 Peter 1:13-16)

Standing Strong In The Midst Of Difficulty

There are many people in this world who are going through hard times whether it is in their finances, in their physical bodies or in their emotions. I've talked to many people on this subject and it never surprises me of the commonality in people's voices; they are all having a difficult time in one of these areas. What we must realize is that it is normal to have problems and trials in our path. It is normal to face difficulties and have heartache as part of our life. It is normal to feel so overwhelmed that you just want to give up, but what I've learned is that when we dig our heels in and stand steadfast determined to overcome that trial, that setback, that heartache, then we will come out of that situation better, wiser and stronger than we were before it. What we must remember is that every problem serves a purpose and every trial is there to help us overcome an area that we are lacking in. Problems can help us to become more patient, more trusting in God, more faithful in prayer, more grateful for our blessings and more appreciative for those closest to us. (James 1:2-4) (Philippians 4:6-7)

It is in facing the problem that we find how strong we really can be. It is in overcoming the trial that we see how much we have learned and benefited because of it. So my best advice if you are going through the darkness is to be of good cheer because before you realize it morning will dawn and joy will be restored. You simply must foresee your end result even while you are still in the pit. Envisioning the end strengthens our heart and reinforces our resolve to never give in and never give up. My philosophy is that if God brings us to it, He will also bring us through it. There is no trial so difficult that God cannot help us to overcome it. Let us simply trust in His perfect plan and know that our end result will be much better, brighter and glorious than any of the former miseries that we overcame. The Lord deserves all the glory for great things He has done and for the great things He is still doing. Trust Him with your life and trust Him even in the midst of your difficulty. The Lord loves you and calls you His beloved child. (1 Thessalonians 5:18) (John 16:33)

Focusing On Our Many Blessings

There are many moments in life when we find ourselves discouraged or downhearted because we focus so much on the physical aspects of life. We look at what we don't have and we find reasons to murmur and complain. We look at our jobs and we wish we had a better position, we look at our finances and we wish we had more in the bank, we look at our health and we wish our situation was better than it is. Our problem isn't in looking at what we don't have, our problem lies in forgetting what we do have. We don't take the time to see the abundance that God has given us. We don't focus on the love that our family gives us which many are not lucky enough to have. We don't see that we had enough food to eat today while many are not as fortunate. We don't realize that the clothes on our back, the roof over our head, the car that we drive are blessings that should be thought upon and shown appreciation for. It is in focusing on our blessings that we see how rich we truly are. Our bank accounts don't need to be full in order for us to be happy and content. We simply must realize that many are not as fortunate as we are. Our gratitude needs to increase because our abundance is much more than we realize. (1 Corinthians 10:10) (Ephesians 1:3-4)

Be encouraged to focus on what you do have. Think of your children, your spouse, your parents, your siblings and your friends. Be thankful for your health, your home, your job. See your many blessings. Be thankful for your legs, your arms, your eyes, your ears. Be glad for the abundance of blessed memories that you can think upon at any time, memories that encourage our hearts, that make us smile and laugh, memories that rekindle hope, memories that bring joy, memories that remind us how loved we are now and have been in times past. See your riches. Focus on your blessings. Do not allow yourself to murmur and complain about the temporary trials in your path. They are not here to stay. What we must remember is that in the end, those trials will make us better, wiser and stronger than we were before them and they will serve a purpose to better our future. (Philippians 2:14-15) (Ephesians 3:20-21)

Remember it is in blessing our today despite its hardships, discouragements and setbacks that we can look for tomorrow with hope. Be encouraged again to bless your days with your words and with your acts. See your glass as half-full and never as half-empty. The Lord is with you and has never left your side. Thank Him for all that He has graciously given to you.

Looking Past Our Imperfections

We should never get down on ourselves when we fall short. Many times we strive for perfection and we do our best to put on a persona that all is well and everything in our life is to our liking. We all know that is not the case. We all have setbacks, we've all fallen short at one time or another and we all need grace in order to stand up again. What we should realize is that it's okay to not be perfect, it's okay to make mistakes, it's okay to fall short, but what is not okay is for us to keep making mistakes and falling short. When we learn from our mistakes, we become wiser so that the same thing won't happen again. When we fail in a certain task, we learn the lesson from that failure and we can rise up stronger for the next task ahead of us. Life is all about learning and becoming better than we were before. We learn the lessons, become better because of them and when we become better, we can help others in areas that we have already learned from. (Romans 3:10-12) (Psalm 84:11)

Be encouraged to love yourself no matter your imperfections. Realize how special you are and remember how much you have to offer. No matter your past shortfalls, you can begin again. With God, a second chance is always available to those who seek Him. He is able to cleanse us of all our unrighteousness, create within us a clean heart and lead our life onto the best path as He sees fit. When we surrender our will and ask for His will to be done, great things will begin to take place in our life. Trust the Lord in every area of your life and know that your ending will be much more blessed and fruitful than your beginnings. Believe it for yourself and strive to achieve it all the days of your life. (Jeremiah 31:3) (1 Corinthians 10:13)

Inspiring Messages

The following messages are written to inspire you to become more than you ever thought you can be. You can brighten your corner, you can change someone's outlook for the better, you can let your light shine in the world and you can make a lasting impact that will never be forgotten or erased. You simply must believe in yourself as God believes in you.

Initiating Good Works

Many times in life we find ourselves being nice or considerate to only those who are nice and considerate towards us. We allow their actions to dictate our reactions. If they treat us kindly, we treat them kindly, if they do something nice for us, we will then do something nice for them. When we act in this manner, we are not allowing ourselves to be the giver of happiness. When we allow others to initiate good things, we are allowing our life to remain stagnant based upon someone else's actions. That ought not to be. We should be the initiators of blessings, joy and happiness. (Romans 12:10) (Matthew 5:43-48)

Our countenance should reflect the joy of the Lord that is in our hearts. One should only look at our demeanor and feel the infectious joy that permeates from within our being. My challenge to you is to allow your life to be the initiator of good things. Say hello to the stranger next to you, share a word of encouragement, smile more for no apparent reason and allow your life to be the catalyst in which the lives of others will be made brighter and better. We do have it within ourselves to make a difference, we just have to make a conscious effort. (James 1:22)

Be encouraged to think on how you can make a difference. See the areas where you can impact someone else. It is so easy to ask someone how their day is going, to say hello more, to smile more and to simply take an interest in someone else. People need to know that they are loved, cared about and thought of. Let us take the reins and be the initiator of doing good works. As children of the Most High God we are to lead by example, we are to love without motive and we are to encourage and lift up those who are downtrodden. When we act in this manner, we will please God and we will bless our neighbor more than we can think or imagine. (Romans 14:19) (Romans 12:9)

Be Of Good Cheer

The Lord has spoken to my heart to write a message focused on one phrase and that is 'Be of Good Cheer'. There are many people who get down and discouraged because of the trials of life and forget the promise of the Lord that victory is promised to come to those who do not lose heart. It is easy for anyone to hear those words Be of Good Cheer and dismiss them by saying, "That's easy for you to say because you don't have my problems." This is not a phrase meant to merely cheer you up, but is a powerful word from the Lord telling us that no matter what happens, we are to remember His promise of victory and because we have; our demeanor will be one of Good Cheer. (Ephesians 3:13) (John 16:33) (Psalm 34:8-9)

The Lord knows that while we are on the earth problems will come. The Lord Jesus never said that because you have believed in Me, you will travel through life on flowery beds of ease. In truth He said, "In the world you will have tribulation; but be of good cheer, I have overcome the world." The Lord made it a point to emphasize that problems will come, but He made a stronger point in telling us that He has overcome the world for us and so our continence should be one of Good Cheer because of this eternal promise. The Bible also reminds us that we are in the world, but not of the world so our Joy should be full at all times because the Lord conquered every problem on the Cross at Calvary when He said "It Is Finished." (John 16:33) (John 15:18-21) (John 19:30)

If you are facing problems that seem too difficult for you to solve, I encourage you to not spend one moment worrying over that situation, but rather invest that valuable energy in confessing your victory and trust in the Lord and know that God is with you and will bring a solution to every bad situation that comes your way. Praise and Thanksgiving in the midst of a problem is sure to discourage the devil's attacks against your life. I believe the Lord tells us to be of good cheer in the midst of our tribulations so that the enemy can see that we are not focused on the visible which is only temporary, but we're focused on the invisible which will last for all eternity. (Proverbs 3:5-6) (Jeremiah 17:7-8)

Be encouraged to lift up your eyes and faith to God and thank Him that He has already been to the place where your victory lies and has called that place to be your own. Never focus on the problem, but focus on the One who has the solution. The next time you are tempted to tell God how big your problem is, I encourage you to go to your problem and tell that obstacle how big your God is. When our faith lines up with the Word of God, that's when the impossible becomes possible and every obstacle that was in our path is supernaturally removed by the power of Almighty God. (Jeremiah 32:17) (Psalm 25:15-21) (Matthew 19:26)

I pray that you have been encouraged to follow the Lord's remedy and Be of Good Cheer no matter what problem is trying to bring you down. By the Blood of the Lamb and the Word of our testimony, we will overcome the devil and raise our hands in victory. We can do so with Cheerful hearts and Praise filled prayers thanking God for where we were and where we are now. To God be all the Glory, Honor and Praise for great things He has done.

Read and meditate on these scriptures:

James 1:2-5 "My brethren, count it all joy when ye fall into divers temptations; Knowing this, that the trying of your faith worketh patience. But let patience have her perfect work, that ye may be perfect and entire, wanting nothing. If any of you lack wisdom, let him ask of God, that giveth to all men liberally, and upbraideth not; and it shall be given him."

Job 5:19-23 "He shall deliver thee in six troubles: yea, in seven there shall no evil touch thee. In famine He shall redeem thee from death: and in war from the power of the sword. Thou shalt be hid from the scourge of the tongue: neither shalt thou be afraid of destruction when it cometh. At destruction and famine thou shalt laugh: neither shalt thou be afraid of the beasts of the earth. For thou shalt be in league with the stones of the field: and the beasts of the field shall be at peace with thee."

Matthew 5:10-12 Jesus declares, "Blessed are they which are persecuted for righteousness' sake: for theirs is the kingdom of heaven. Blessed are ye, when men shall revile you, and persecute you, and shall say all manner of evil against you falsely, for My sake. Rejoice, and be exceeding glad: for great is your reward in heaven: for so persecuted they the prophets which were before you."

All of these scriptures can be found in the King James Version Bible.

There Are No Coincidences With God

We should always trust that God has our best interest in mind at all times. No matter the trials, tribulations and setbacks of life, we should remain confident that our life is secure in the Hands of the Lord. When we have an unwavering trust that God is with us, then nothing will be able to make us lose our peace or make us question God's plan for our life. Many times things happen that we don't understand and we think that God has forgotten us or even worse He has forsaken us, but what we fail to see in those instances is that He is working things for our good in the end. The road that we're traveling on is long and we can't see the end result of it, but God can. He sees every pitfall, every detour, every crack in the road and in His infinite wisdom, He works out all of those temporary setbacks for our ultimate benefit. (Isaiah 49:15-16) (Romans 8:28)

Every setback and every crack in the road that we think is too difficult to endure is serving a purpose. It is teaching us a lesson, it is strengthening our resolve, it is giving us wisdom, knowledge, patience and understanding that a straight and trouble-free road could never give us. Let us see every trial as a blessing. Let us see every detour as an opportunity to learn something new. Many have said that the Lord works in mysterious ways and He does. He saves us at just the right moment. He is never too early and He has yet to be late. In those instances that we think everything worked out perfectly and we give credit to coincidence, that is just God showing up right on time giving us our hearts desire. (James 1:2-5) (Job 23:10-12)

Be encouraged to thank the Lord for the many coincidences in your life. Thank Him for being there for you when you didn't realize it. Thank Him for answering your prayers in His own perfect way not giving us what we want, but more importantly giving us what we need. The Lord is good. His ways are perfect. He loves us to no end and the sooner we realize these truths, the quicker we will be in calling upon Him all the days of our life.

Doing Our Jobs With Excellence

We should always be appreciative and thankful for the jobs that we have. Many times we are tempted to murmur and complain because we either find our jobs too difficult or too routine. What we must realize is that when we do our jobs with excellence, we are preparing ourselves to reach greater heights. Whatever our job may be, we should do it with all of our heart, mind and soul. We should put in every effort to get the best results that we possibly can. Whether that means going to work early or having to stay late, we should do what is necessary to get the best results possible. The work that we do is a direct reflection of who we are on the inside. When we put in the extra effort, spend the extra time and go the extra mile, we are showing that we are faithful and determined to do our absolute best. When we do our absolute best that is when we prepare ourselves for promotion. Giving our all regardless of the job at hand shows our strong character and our unwavering integrity. (Colossians 3:23-24) (Job 31:6)

Giving our all should be a plan of action for every job that we are lucky enough to have. It doesn't matter if you are a stay-at-home parent, a secretary, a sanitary worker or a CEO of a company. We should do the jobs that we are blessed enough to have with joy and excellence. When we take pride in our work, it will no longer seem like a job, but it will be a part of who we are on the inside. We are to look at the work that we do and see it as an extension of ourselves. When we put our whole heart into something that we're doing, then the results will come forth that much greater. (Ephesians 6:5-8)

If you are finding yourself feeling discouraged because you don't like your job, I would encourage you to reevaluate how you see it. Don't look at it as a means to an end, but see it for what it can be. See your job as an extension of yourself. See the job that you do as a responsibility and not a burden. See the good in the work that you do. See the benefits that you gain from your work and see the benefits that you offer to others because of your work. When we see the benefits of our jobs, the blessings that come from it and the responsibilities that we have in doing it to our best ability, we will begin to really appreciate the work that we've been doing.

Sometimes all we need is a little perspective to see how blessed we really are. Be encouraged to see all that you have been blessed with and do all that you can to continue doing the work that you have been fortunate enough to have with excellence.

Blessing Yourself By Blessing Others

We should never put so much emphasis on gaining the material possessions of this world only for our vanity to be satisfied. What we must realize and remind ourselves is that life is temporary and the things associated with it will one day pass away. Striving for self gain will leave one's heart feeling empty no matter how many possessions surround them. Material things don't make the man, but a heart seeking God's will and trying our best to act in a manner that is pleasing to Him will satisfy our souls and will fill our hearts with a Joy that is unimaginable. Living only for yourself will not bring lasting satisfaction to your life, but striving to be of use to someone else and trying to better their life will bless you beyond comprehension. (Genesis 3:19) (James 4:14) (Isaiah 6:8)

I am a firm believer in sowing and reaping. I believe that whatever I put into the ground will come back one day to either bless or curse my life. When I sow goodness, charity, love, encouragement and hope than I should expect to reap those same blessings that I imparted into someone else's life. Whatever good you do to someone else will come back to you. The opposite is also true. Whatever strife you cause, hatred you impart or evil that you do will come back to you one day. We will receive the same things that we give out so let us recognize the importance of sowing goodness into our own lives and into the lives of those around us. (Galatians 6:7-10) (2 Corinthians 9:6-8)

I know many of us can think back over our life and see that decades have passed that seem like only a few short years ago and it is for this reason that we should focus on using our life to make a difference that will never be erased. Doing good lasts forever no matter who the good is done to. It may be a family member, a friend or a complete stranger. The good works that are done do not matter who they are done to because the same result will come forth regardless. If you're blessing someone you know or someone you don't know, your memory will remain alive in their hearts for the rest of their life. No good deed goes forgotten and every blessing given will be returned multiplied back to you in ways that you've never thought of.

Always remember and keep in mind that when you do something good for someone else, the same will be done for you in your time of need. You are ensuring your own life's success when you act in a manner that is loving, kind, charitable and encouraging. I encourage you to think on how you portray yourself. Are you doing the things that are necessary to bless your own future or are you only interested in what you can gain from others? If you are in the latter category, I strongly encourage you to change your ways. It's not too late to start afresh and lead your life in a manner that is pleasing to the Lord. We never see a millionaire on his deathbed clinching to his riches, but rather what's most important to them at that time are the people that they love the most. Material things don't love back, but the relationships that we nurture, cultivate and bless will love us for the rest of our life and for the rest of theirs.

<u>Never Giving Up On Ourselves</u>

It is important that we have a vision of victory for our life. The path that our life will take has much to do with the vision that we have deep in our hearts and the passion that we have to pursue it. Many times people give up on believing for greater things for their life because of the setbacks that have kept them where they are. They believe that because of their past failures, mistakes and shortfalls that they can never reach towards the heights of victory that they once thought was within their grasp. They give up on believing for greater things. They settle for where they are and they believe the lie that this is all that they are meant to be in life. What they must realize is that we all fall down and we all fall short. There is no one person that is perfect, flawless and without blemish. We all fall flat on our face at one time or another, but the important thing is getting back up and believing that a second chance is available to us. (Proverbs 29:18) (Jeremiah 33:3) (Habakkuk 2:2-3)

No matter what we have gone through and no matter what we have faced, as long as we hold on to the dreams that are in our hearts and be determined to pursue them with all of our might, then we will see that greatness is still ahead of us. There is no has been when it comes to God. As long as we keep Him at the center of our life, then a new beginning, a new chance and a revived dream can begin to be fulfilled. Never think that you are beyond redemption or that you have reached your fullest potential. The Lord is never finished with us. A new thing is always dawning. We simply must believe that we are meant for more. We have to forgive ourselves for our past and see that a new beginning is available through God's forgiveness, His redemption and His ability to birth within us a renewed vision for our life. (Psalm 37:4-6) (Ezekiel 36:26)

Be encouraged to see that you have much to offer this world. Do not let yourself give up when things don't look their best, but be determined to weather the storm and come out of it better than you were before. The struggles of life serve many purposes. They strengthen our resolve, they teach us patience, they equip us with wisdom and knowledge and they show us who we really are deep down. Use your past experiences to your benefit. Teach others what you have learned, do now with what you know what you couldn't do before. Pray and seek the Lord to show you what you are to do in life if you aren't sure. The Lord is faithful to hear and answer our prayers when we seek Him. Never think that you are abandoned or forsaken. With God a new beginning is always possible. That is how great His love is for you. (Isaiah 55:6-9) (Hebrews 13:5-6)

Following Your Imagination

I hope you are doing well and are in the best of health. I pray that you are rejoicing in this day that God has created and blessing His name for keeping you alive in this beautiful day in time. We must be quick to realize that to be alive in this day is a privilege that the Saints of old could have only wished for. Even with the troubles, heartaches and setbacks, we must see that we are a privileged people who have both been given much and are required of much also. The Lord has gifted each of us in varying ways and calls us to stand in the authority that He has given us through His Word to live a life of victory and triumph to become all who He has made us to be. You are not ordinary, but are a child of God who is special and called to accomplish great things in life. (Jeremiah 31:3)

I recently watched a story about a man named Gustavo Dudamel. Gustavo is a world renowned music conductor who was born in Venezuela. He is known in all circles where classical music is involved and yet he is only 32 years old. Some might say he is a musical genius. Gustavo started taking music lessons at age 4, he conducted his first orchestra at age 12, he was named conductor of Venezuela's National Youth Orchestra at age 15 and at only 28 years old the Los Angeles Philharmonic hired him as their next music director. I believe those are some great accomplishments for someone who is still so young, but if you see and adapt for yourself how this gifted person thinks, you will say to yourself I can do similar things in areas that I am gifted. (Romans 12:4-8) (1 Corinthians 12:12-31)

The interview for the program was filmed mostly in Vienna, Austria and when the interviewer asked Gustavo if he had conducted The Vienna Philharmonic ever before, Gustavo's answer really stayed with me. Gustavo answered, "This is the first time that I am conducting this orchestra for real, but I have been conducting since I was a kid in my mind over and over and over again. In my imagination I have conducted many concerts. Only this time it is for real." The thing that is so special about Gustavo Dudamel is that he has realized the secret to success is found in the imagination. What we imagine to do is what we will bring to pass. The seeds of our imagination will eventually become the fruit and realization of that dream or imagination. (Matthew 17:20) (Proverbs 23:7) (Galatians 6:4-7)

There is a powerful story in the Bible concerning man's imagination. You may know the story of the Tower of Babel where men gathered themselves together and decided to build a tower so high that it would reach into the heavens. The story is found in Genesis 11:1-10, but I want to share a brief excerpt from verses 4-7 "And they said, Go to, let us build us a city and a tower, whose top may reach unto heaven; and let us make us a name, lest we be scattered abroad upon the face of the whole earth. And the LORD came down to see the city and the tower, which the children of men builded. And the LORD said, Behold, the people is one, and they have all one language; and this they begin to do: and now nothing will be restrained from them, which they have imagined to do." The Lord Himself said that 'nothing will be restrained from them which they have imagined to do.' In other words, what they think in their mind is so powerful that nothing can keep them from fulfilling and accomplishing what they first imagined to do.

Of course it wasn't God's will for them to succeed and in order to stop them the Lord confounded their language so that one person would not be able to understand another person. Now for us in this day and time that love the Lord and want to do His will, we need to gird ourselves up and imagine the life that we want for ourselves. We must imagine and see ourselves blessed and highly favored. We are to see ourselves successful, healthy, blessed, prosperous, whole, encouraged, above only and not beneath, lending to many people and not borrowing. The picture that we see for ourselves is the picture that will eventually come to life. (Deut. 28:12-14)

How do you see yourself? Do you see yourself with a family? Do you see yourself in a successful job? Do you see yourself healthy and whole? This is not a matter of positive thinking, but it is a rule of God that whatever you imagine for yourself and pursue wholeheartedly is what will come to pass in your life. You must believe in yourself as God believes in you and not doubt the gifts and talents that have been instilled within your heart. You must nurture your ability and see yourself succeeding. You must imagine in your mind what you would like your future to be. In which job position, on which stage, in which area of life, etc. What are you imagining about your life? (2 Corinthians 9:8) (2 Chronicles 16:9)

God said nothing will be restrained from them which they have imagined to do. Imagine for yourself great things; even things that you can't believe will come true. Think and imagine bigger than you have ever done before and use your faith to believe for what you have not believed for in the past. Always remember that our God can do the impossible, but He will not move unless faith is first put into action. One of my favorite scriptures is found in Hebrews 11:1 "Now faith is the substance of things hoped for, the evidence of things not seen." I encourage you again to imagine.

Do exactly as Gustavo Dudamel has done and see yourself victorious and triumphant. Allow the seeds of your imagination to take root so that in due time those seeds will grow and mature and will finally bring into realization what first started with a simple image in your mind. Praise the Lord that He has given us every tool necessary to live an overcoming, abundant and blessed life in Him. (Galatians 6:9) (John 14:15-19)

Read and meditate on these scriptures:

2 Chronicles 16:9 "For the eyes of the LORD run to and fro throughout the whole earth, to shew Himself strong in the behalf of them whose heart is perfect toward Him..."

Romans 8:31-32 "What shall we then say to these things? If God be for us, who can be against us? He that spared not His own Son, but delivered Him up for us all, how shall He not with Him also freely give us all things?"

Matthew 21:21-22 Jesus says, "…Verily I say unto you, If ye have faith, and doubt not, ye shall not only do this which is done to the fig tree, but also if ye shall say unto this mountain, Be thou removed, and be thou cast into the sea; it shall be done. And all things, whatsoever ye shall ask in prayer, believing, ye shall receive."

All of these scriptures can be found in the King James Version Bible.

Holding On To Hope

One thing we should never ever let go of is hope. We have to hold on to hope no matter what we face in life. No matter the trials, tribulations, setbacks or failures, if we hold on to hope then we will be strong enough to face every problem with a deep knowing that God is in control and our story isn't finished yet. Hope is kind of like faith in that you have to hold on to it in the darkest of times having a deep sense of confidence that all will be well in the end. Hope encourages us to believe that a brighter day is coming. Hope strengthens us to believe that God's omniscience will lead us onto the best path. Hope lifts up our spirits keeping us from giving up when that's all we want to do. (Psalm 16:8-11) (Lamentations 3:24-27)

No matter what comes your way, keep hope and faith at the center of your life. Believe that greater things are coming your way. Never doubt that the darkest times serve a purpose to make you stronger, wiser and better than you were before. When we have hope and faith alive in our hearts then nothing will be able to bring down our spirits. We will see the good in every situation. We will focus on our blessings despite the temptation to murmur and complain about our problems. We will see our glass as half-full and not half empty. Having hope makes us look forward to a better tomorrow despite the bleakness that we may be seeing today. Be encouraged to let God know that your hope is in Him. (Psalm 130:5-7) (Psalm 119:10-12)

Thank the Lord for every gift and every blessing that He has graciously given to you and remember His goodness when times of testing tempt you to give up. The Lord is not finished with you yet. That's the great thing about our God; in Him there is always a second chance. Stay hopeful and never even think of giving up.

Having The Right Attitude In The Tough Times

"Things could always be worse." That's what I tell myself whenever I feel like complaining about the trials in my path. I guess it's my way of being thankful that the situation I'm in isn't as difficult as the trials and tribulations that many others go through. Sometimes we just have to appreciate our "burden" and learn to look on the bright side of things. It is easy for anyone to have a pity party and have a "woe is me" attitude, but when we take the time to see our many blessings, we will remember how blessed and fortunate we really are. Looking at our glass as half empty does nothing to rejuvenate and reinvigorate our spirit because we will continually focus on what we are missing rather than seeing all that we possess. We must remember how fortunate we really are despite our hardships and be quick to speak words of thanksgiving, gratitude and praise for all that God has given us. (Psalm 142:4-7) (Psalm 121:1-8)

We should never expect only good to come our way because it is in the trials that we become strengthened, empowered and built up for our future. Some see the bad times as only that. They murmur, complain and wish their burden wasn't so heavy without realizing the purpose of that burden. When we take a moment to see the lessons that we've learned in times past for the trials that we overcame, we can begin to appreciate the new trials in our path and realize that they do serve a purpose. Having the correct attitude has much to do with the final outcome. When we get it deep in our minds that we will become better, wiser and stronger at the end of our trial, then we will face it with a renewed vigor and determination and with a deep knowing that it is serving a purpose to make us more than we were before. (John 16:33) (James 1:2-5)

I encourage you to have a good and right attitude despite your trial and hardship. Whatever your situation may be whether it is physical, financial or emotional, face it with a renewed fervor that you will become better in the end because of that situation. Tell yourself that your situation is serving a purpose to help you and equip you to face any situation that may come your way in the future. I encourage you again to rejoice and be exceedingly glad in the midst of your trial. Let God know that your eyes of faith are not focused on the physical, but they are focused on the Eternal God who is able to bring our answers in ways that we have never thought of or imagined. (2 Corinthians 4:16-18) (Ephesians 3:20-21)

Praise the Lord for the Joy that He gives in the midst of difficulty!

Being A Burden Bearer

We should always take the initiative to be uplifting, comforting and encouraging towards those who are facing difficult times in their life. We must realize that many people whether they are our family, friends, co-workers or acquaintances face difficult situations and they need to be reassured that others are there for them to help, strengthen and lift them up when they feel that they are at their weakest. As believers in Christ we are to lead by example and act in a manner that would be pleasing to our Father in Heaven. Comforting the brokenhearted and showing them that love abounds will encourage their hearts and will show them that they are never alone and that others are there for them in their time of need. Just as we would want someone to help carry our burden and comfort us in our time of need, let us be their burden bearer and show them how loved they are and how much they mean to us. (1 Thessalonians 5:11-13) (Hebrews 10:24-25)

In the end, all that we will have is what we did to help someone else. Our legacy will never fade and our memory will live on in the hearts of those whom we've helped in times past. Be encouraged to see the value in helping others in their time of need. Put yourself in their position and just as you would wish for someone to do for you, you can do the same for them. The Lord Jesus declares in Matthew 22:37-40 "Thou shalt love the Lord thy God with all thy heart, and with all thy soul, and with all thy mind.

This is the first and great commandment. And the second is like unto it, Thou shalt love thy neighbour as thyself. On these two commandments hang all the law and the prophets." Let us love our neighbor as we love ourselves.

Recognizing Those Who've Helped Us

It is important that we remember and recognize those who have helped us and been there for us in times past. There are many people that we've come across during our lifetime that have done so much to teach us, encourage us, inspire us, lift us up and let us know how special we are and how much we have to offer this world. Those who have given of themselves selflessly deserve our recognition for all that they have done for us. By giving people the praise and credit that they deserve, we are encouraging their hearts to know that they made a difference and with our thanks we are showing them our appreciation and gratitude for helping to make us better, wiser and stronger than we were before. (Proverbs 15:23) (Proverbs 3:27-28)

Just as we would like to be thanked for being helpful, let us remember those who have done so much for us and give them the attention they deserve. It may be a teacher, a co-worker, a relative, a spouse or a friend. When we know in our hearts that they made a difference in our lives, we should take the initiative and show our thankfulness. Giving thanks can be done in many ways. We can buy them a gift, treat them to lunch, write a heartfelt letter or we can sit down with them and share point by point what they did to bless our life. You may not think doing this is a big deal or that you don't have enough time to do it, but I encourage you to see the importance of giving credit to those who were there for you when you needed them. (John 13:34-35) (Romans 12:9-10)

I can remember doing this not too long ago to a friend of mine who was there for me during a difficult time in my life. She didn't know it at the time, but she helped to encourage, inspire and lift me up when I needed it the most. That was nearly 15 years ago and as I was remembering her kindness not too long ago, I thought it would be good to let her know how much I appreciate her kindness. I wrote her a short letter, maybe three paragraphs writing in detail what she did for me and how much I appreciated her kindness.

I thanked her and told her that I would never forget her. My recognition of her selflessness was a very simple thing to do, but it meant so much to her. She responded very modestly thanking me and telling me how touched she was by the letter and she ended the letter by saying "As you will not forget me, I will not forget you..." I know my heart was happy for recognizing her kindness and thanking her for it and I know that others will be just as touched and encouraged when you tell them the difference they have made in your life.

Be encouraged to think on the many people who have made a difference in your life and make an extra effort to show your gratitude and appreciation. It may take you a little time, but it will be the best investment of time that you can make.

Being A Beacon Of Hope

The generosity that comes from our hearts and is passed on to the hearts of others is something that will never be forgotten. What we must remember about life is that it is fleeting. We can be here one moment and gone the next and all we will have left on this Earth is what we did to help others become better. When we see someone in need and do something to help their situation, we are ministering to them physically, emotionally and spiritually. When we give to someone in need, we are showing them that love abounds, we are encouraging their hearts to never give up and we are acting as ambassadors of God bringing light to a dark situation. People simply need to know that others care for their well-being and when we act as Christ did while He was on the Earth, we are following His command to treat others as we would like to be treated. (Ephesians 4:29) (Galatians 6:10)

A quote that I love by Charles Spurgeon says "A good character is the best tombstone. Those who loved you and were helped by you will remember you. Carve your name on hearts, not on marble." No matter how great our own difficulties are, we still have the ability to be encouragers. We may not have the greatest of wealth, we may not be able to give as much as we'd like, but when we do something kind for someone else despite our own hardships, we will make an impact that is inconceivable in our own minds. God is able to take the smallest of pebbles and use it to create the biggest of ripples. We simply must surrender ourselves so that we can be used to make that ripple that will never be forgotten. Be encouraged to be that tower that sheds light in every direction. Allow your life to impact the lives of others by giving, helping, encouraging and challenging all people to believe in themselves again and showing them how special they are in God's eyes.

Letting Go Of The Guilt

There are many people in this world who find that their life is hindered because of some mistake that they made in the past that they can't put behind them. They have a sense of guilt that lies deep within their heart and they can't let it go, forgive themselves and move forward in life. What we must always remember and recognize is that guilt is like an invisible chain that can keep our life locked up, and in turn we become stagnant and unproductive. What we must do is rest in God's forgiveness and realize that if God forgave us for our past shortfalls, then we should also forgive ourselves and move forward in life reaching the goals and desires that were once so evident in our hearts. Having feelings of constant guilt does not come from the Lord. The Bible says that God wishes for us to be at peace, to be filled with hope and to rest in His forgiveness. The enemy is the one who wants us to relive our past mistakes and he is the one who reminds us of our shortfalls trying to make us believe the lie that we are unworthy to move ahead in life. (John 14:27) (Matthew 11:28-30) (John 8:44)

When we realize that God's forgiveness covers our past, we will no longer be stuck in the rut of the past, but we will be reinvigorated to face each new day with hope, joy and zeal. Living in the past only hinders our future. When we constantly remember our past mistakes and shortfalls, we will be discouraged, disheartened and unable to move forward to reach the heights of victory that are in our future. We are in essence canceling the blessings ahead because we are so focused on the mistakes of the past. Our feelings of guilt keeps us locked up even though God has given us the key to be free. He wishes for us to rest in Him, but that is solely in our hands. (Genesis 41:51) (Matthew 16:19) (Psalm 116:5-9)

Be encouraged to look forward in life. Let go of the guilt, forget the past and start living for your future. If you have confessed your sins to the Lord and asked Him to forgive you, then you have a clean slate and an unlimited future in God's eyes. Rest in His forgiveness and learn to love life again. Don't focus on the past. Let the past stay there and look ahead towards a brighter day with new hopes, new dreams and new joys. You can do it because with God all things are possible. (Isaiah 1:18) (Luke 18:27)

Enjoying Your Life Today

There are moments in life when we rush through our days in anticipation of some event that is yet to take place in our future. We wait for our tomorrow's with eagerness without appreciating and utilizing this day to its fullest potential. We sometimes sit by in boredom because we don't realize how special this day really is. We don't see its beauty, we don't see its potential, we don't see all that we can do with it. Instead of rejoicing in this day and enjoying every bit of it, we wait for tomorrow without realizing that we may never see it. The Bible tells us in Psalm 118:24 "This is the day the Lord has made, we will rejoice and be glad in it." We are to see the beauty that surrounds us, we are to encourage, inspire, challenge and lift up all those around us who need to be ministered to, we are to bless this day and let it know that we were here. (Psalm 34:1-8) (Proverbs 27:1)

We must each realize that our life is important. It should be used up. Don't go to your grave with mileage unused. Don't die without reaching your fullest potential. Whatever your job in life is, do it with excellence and with eagerness. Don't wait for tomorrow to be happy and to start enjoying life. You have today to see the beauty that surrounds you. Ask the Lord to open your eyes to see what you haven't seen before. Make it a goal every day to focus for a minute or two on a flower, a tree, a sunset, anything that can reinvigorate and rejuvenate your zest for life.

When we focus on the blessings that surround us, we will be quick to appreciate our life and all that we have been lucky enough to possess. Sometimes all we need is a little perspective to see how fortunate we really are. I encourage you to bless this day with your life and do not let it pass you by unused. Live, Love, Laugh and Enjoy your life today!

<u>Staying Faithful In The Midst of Uncertainty</u>

It is easy to become discouraged when we try over and over to find our place in life unsuccessfully. What we must remember is that while we are alive God has a plan and purpose for us to fulfill. We may not know what it is in this present time, but if we continually seek the Lord and ask for His wisdom and guidance, the Lord is faithful to lead us onto the path of our destiny. Never become discouraged when uncertain times come your way, but rather use that opportunity to show your confidence in the Lord knowing that God has something special waiting for you just ahead. (Jeremiah 33:3)

Be encouraged to praise God even in the midst of the hardship showing the Lord that your unwavering faith is focused on Him and not on the negative situation before you. God moves mountains for those who stand in faith believing so take courage and show your confidence in Him. (Isaiah 55:6-9)

Being Someone's Visible Angel

It is a great blessing to know that we can be used by the Lord to lighten the burden of those who mean so much to us. Many times we feel compelled to be helpful towards someone else and we really don't know why; our heart simply tells us that is what we need to do right now. I believe the Lord leads us in this way so that others may be helped and shown the love that they needed to feel in that moment. What we must remember and keep in mind is that we are all connected in this world. Even if we are not related, we are still connected. We are all created by the Lord and are called to be there for one another in times of need. When we take those opportunities that come before us to be helping, to be encouraging, to show that we care, I believe we are taking the place of Angels for those few moments. The Angels that people can see. What are Angels anyway? They are beings created to intervene, to help, to strengthen, to bring good news and to shed light on a dark situation. We can take that position when we feel inclined to do so and use our gifts to be a blessing to someone in need. (Galatians 6:2) (James 1:27)

The Bible tells us in Galatians 6:10 "As we have therefore opportunity, let us do good unto all men, especially unto them who are of the household of faith." We are to do good unto all men. Doing good comes in many forms. It can be a listening ear, a helping hand, a motivational speech, a forgiving heart and the list continues on. Just as we would like to have someone be there for us in our time of need, let us remember to be there for someone else in their time of need. The gifts that we give will be remembered far longer by the recipients than they ever will be by us. I'm sure many of us can remember when a good deed was done for us. We don't forget the goodness of others and they won't forget our intervention either. Be encouraged to take on the mentality of being an Angel here on Earth. Using your life to benefit someone else ensures your immortality in their minds and hearts. What a great legacy we will leave when all we will be remembered for is the good that we did for others. That is a legacy we can each be proud of. (Luke 6:31-36) (Ephesians 6:5-8)

Being Our Brother's Keeper

With the many pressures and stresses that people go through on a daily basis, they sometimes need a word of encouragement to let them know that all will be well in the end. What we must remember is that in life all we have is the love of our friends and family. We are each other's backbone and when one of us is in need, we should be quick to lend a helping hand and reassure them that they have our support for whatever they may need. It is easy for anyone to feel down or discouraged when the weight of the world seems to be laying on their shoulders, but if they know that others care about their well-being and wish to help carry their burden, they will feel a lot less stress and they will know how greatly loved they truly are. (Matthew 22:37-39) (Philippians 2:2-8)

No matter what we go through in life, we can use a word of encouragement to lift up our spirits. Whether they are financial problems, relationship problems, health issues or stress from difficult situations, we can do our part to lighten the load of those who mean the most to us. We can let them know that every bump in the road serves a purpose and every trial that comes our way will make us better than we were before it. We can encourage those who are heavy laden to never give up and always believe that they will overcome any situation and be better in the end because of that hardship. Let us always be quick to encourage the downhearted and show them that their glass is not half empty, but rather it is more than half full and on its way to overflowing. A negative situation is never made better by dwelling on it, but rather that situation can be used to elevate our life to greater heights when we use our energy to see the good that can come from that situation. (1 John 4:10-12) (Romans 15:1-2)

I encourage you to be quick to lift other's up, to shed light on a dark situation and to bring encouragement to those who need to be ministered to. All that we have learned and witnessed throughout our life can be used to minister grace to those around us and to let them know that we love them and will be there for them no matter what comes their way. The Lord Jesus says it best in Luke 6:30 "And as ye would that men should do to you, do ye also to them likewise."

Being There For One Another

It is important that we value the relationships that mean the most to us. There are many moments in life when we become too busy to pay attention to our loved ones and show them how much we really care about their feelings as well as their well-being. We may be distracted by any number of things and because of this those closest to us may feel neglected, ignored or even abandoned. What we must realize is that just as we would like to be attended to and shown love and respect, it is the same with those around us. They want to be shown that they are loved, appreciated and cared about and when we don't take time to ask about their day, take a general interest in what they're doing and simply be there to give and take in conversation, then they will feel let down in that area of our relationships. (Galatians 6:10) (Luke 6:31)

One thing we must remember is that our relationships are the most important thing in our lives. Without the love of our family and friends, how much meaning would life have? Who would we go to in our time of need if we don't have our loved ones? They are most important and deserve our attention. They deserve our love and respect. No matter how busy we may get, we can set those "important things" aside for a little while to take an interest in those who mean the most to us. We can ask about their day, see if anything is bothering them and show by our actions how greatly loved and appreciated they really are.

It may not seem like a big deal to us to ask how someone is doing, but to them, it can mean a lot.

Let this message encourage you to take time for those whom you love. Pay extra attention to them, show that you are genuinely interested in what they're doing and simply be the catalyst to strengthen your relationships and show those who mean the most to you that they are greatly appreciated, loved and thought upon. When we do the simple things for our loved ones, they will be encouraged, lifted up and reinvigorated to face whatever may come their way. We strengthen one another with our love. We motivate one another by cheering each other on and with our positive actions we let those closest to us know that we will be there for them no matter what comes their way and no matter how busy we may sometimes get. (Ecclesiastes 4:9-12)

I encourage you again to take time for your loved ones and nurture the relationships that mean the most to you. The seeds that you sow now will grow and come back to bless you again one day.

Showing Kindness To Others

The word kindness has been repeating in my mind lately and I have been thinking about the many ways that we can sow kindness in the lives of others. One thing we must always remember is that everyone around us is fighting some kind of battle. They might have health issues, financial issues, emotional issues, mental stresses or any other number of things that we as humans go through in life. And it is for this reason that we take on the mentality to be kind at all times. If someone says something rude to us, does something to offend as or they are simply not treating us right, we can respond with kindness. We don't have to be rude in return. We don't have to do an eye for an eye and a tooth for a tooth. As God's children, we are to return good for evil. We are to return kindness for rudeness. We are to sow love in the midst of being shown hate. We must remember that when people try to hurt us, it is because they themselves are hurting. They are not happy in their own lives and they don't have the capacity to show the same love that we offer. You must remember that love conquers all. Love wins in the end. No matter how opposed they may seem to our kindness, deep down they will remember it and think on it in their quiet time. (Matthew 5:7-12) (Matthew 5:38-48)

The Lord Jesus declares in Matthew 5:44-45 "Love your enemies, bless them that curse you, do good to them that hate you, and pray for them which despitefully use you, and persecute you; That ye may be the children of your

Father which is in heaven: for He maketh His sun to rise on the evil and on the good, and sendeth rain on the just and on the unjust." We who have given our lives to the Lord and have been committed in serving God any way we can are to remember this command. We are to bless, forgive, pray for, and help heal all those who are hurting around us. We are to sow kindness, sow love, sow mercy, sow forgiveness and simply treat others as we would like to be treated. How can we begin? We can do simple things to show our love. We can buy our coworker lunch for no apparent reason. We can buy our loved ones a gift to show how much they mean to us. We can spend time with that one who is feeling discouraged or depressed and show them that somebody cares for their well-being. Mercy and love are shown in many different ways, but our main goal is to make sure it is shown. As long as the intent is pure and without motive then it should be done. (Romans 12:9-10)

Be encouraged to take on the mentality of being kind no matter how strong the temptation is to return rudeness when someone isn't treating you right. Take the higher road and sow mercy. You will quickly find how being an example of light and love will change those around you. They will have seen what true love is and how it can be a part of their own life. The only way people change is to be convicted in their heart. When they see the error of their ways and they come to the realization that there is a better way; that is when they will seek forgiveness and see the mercy and love of the Lord. May we each practice kindness and mercy each day that we have left on this earth.

Making The Most Of Each New Day

With the unpredictability of life we should never postpone for tomorrow what can be done today. There are many people in this world who place their happiness on hold because they are waiting for some event to take place first before they can fully enjoy life. They wait for their health to be restored, for their finances to get better, for their children to finish preschool, elementary school, high school, etc. before they can enjoy life and do the things that bring happiness, laughter and joy. What we must realize is that tomorrow is not promised to us and by waiting for tomorrow, we are missing the blessing of today. We should remember the frailty of life and use each day to its fullest to better ourselves, to accomplish goals, to bless others and to simply be in the moment and realize how blessed we are and how much we have to be thankful for. That is what life is all about. It is about growing, learning and becoming better than we were before. When we realize the true meaning of life, we will stop postponing our happiness and be happy right now. (James 4:13-14)

In the midst of the trial we will smile. In the midst of the difficulty we will give God praise. In the midst of the struggle we will be happy. As long as God is on His Throne then all is well. We shouldn't become anxious, struggle or fear what the future holds. As long as we remember Who holds the future, we should rest confidently and do our best to enjoy life to its fullest. No worry, no fear, no heartache. Be happy with all that God has given you and remember the many blessings that you've received in times past. Sometimes it's easy to complain about the trials before us because we forget of the many blessings that have already crossed our path. When we remember how fortunate we've been, it is easier to bless God and thank Him for all that He has done for us. A thankful heart will be a receptive heart. Let us remember to give God thanks, to rest in His ability to meet our needs and to do our best to be at peace and enjoy life right now to the full. (Psalm 16:7-9) (Psalm 26:11-12)

Today Is A Great Day

We are to always keep in mind that today is the best day of our lives. No matter the struggles or hardships that come our way, we are to see the good in every situation and do our best to get the most out of what we've been given. It is easy to think that our happiness and sense of peace lies somewhere in the future, and in a certain moment of time we will be content and completely fulfilled in our life. We need to realize that in this day is where our happiness lies and where our peace is waiting to be received. (2 Timothy 3:14-17)

Jesus says in John 14:27 "Peace I leave with you, my peace I give unto you: not as the world giveth, give I unto you. Let not your heart be troubled, neither let it be afraid." The Lord who has worked all things out for our good wants for us to stand in our peace and know that He has well-equipped us to prosper and be blessed in this day. The Bible says in Psalm 118:24 "This is the day which the LORD hath made; we will rejoice and be glad in it." Be encouraged to see the good and know that within your spirit lies every tool that is required for you to receive and rest in your peace, joy and contentment. (John 16:23-24) (1 Timothy 6:6-8)

Doing Our Job With Excellence

We should never see our life as insignificant or less than simply because we haven't accomplished great things yet. What we should always remember and keep in mind is that God has instilled great dreams and aspirations within each of our hearts that are meant to be realized and fulfilled. The Lord has never created anything without a set purpose behind it. From the smallest of creatures to His greatest creations; each has a set plan and purpose behind it. When we believe this truth and know that we are meant for more, that is when we can begin to see how worthy we are in God's eyes and how great His love is for us. Many times we want to be used in extraordinary ways to make a difference that will impact multitudes, but we don't know how or where to begin. What I have found to be true is to simply do the work before me with care and excellence. Whatever job I have at the moment, I should do it as if The President is going to come and check after me to see how I did. Doing the job before us as though it is the most important thing is what excels us to greater heights. (Romans 8:31-37)

Be encouraged to take on the mentality of being excellent in your work. Whatever your job is, do it to the best of your ability. Whether you are a homemaker, a teacher, an engineer or a CEO, be excellent in your work. Do your job with care, with pride and with love and because you do, you will be rewarded. Doing good brings its own reward in its own way. When we care about the simple things, the bigger things tend to work themselves out to our benefit. Believe in yourself and know that you are well able to be excellent in your work. The job that God has given you is yours to excel at. Be happy in it, be proud of it and be excellent at it. (2 Timothy 4:5) (Ecclesiastes 9:10)

Helping Others Carry Their Burden

With so many people struggling and having a hard time around us, we are to remember to be there for them letting them know that everything will be all right. We should always take the initiative and be comforting towards those who are down or discouraged. We as God's stewards must comfort the brokenhearted and be their shoulder to lean upon. The Bible declares in 1 Thessalonians 5:11 "Therefore comfort each other and edify one another..." The word edify means to build up. We are told to comfort one another and build others up so that they might believe in themselves again and know how valuable they really are. It is easy for anyone to turn their head and ignore the hardships of others, but as true believers in Christ we are called to lift up, to strengthen, to encourage, to love others and to esteem them higher than we esteem ourselves. (James 1:27) (Philippians 2:3-7)

Just as we would love to have someone to comfort us in our time of trouble, we should be quick to offer that same love and compassion to those in need around us. We are to comfort them with our words and with our actions. Giving an encouraging word can do so much to reaffirm their belief in themselves and show them that life is worth living and that their life means so much to so many people including ourselves. Be encouraged to be that rock that others can lean upon. Give an encouraging word, do a kind deed, treat others the way you would like to be treated and do for them what they can't do for themselves right now. By being a comforter, we are following Christ's example of loving others and showing them the love of God that dwells within our hearts. (1 Thessalonians 5:14-15)

Trusting The Lord No Matter What

It is easy to murmur and complain when tough times come our way, but if we change our mindset and keep our eyes focused on the Lord, then we will remain confident in His ability to deliver us no matter what comes our way. Our job as believers in the Lord is to remain in confidence and trust that God will meet our every need no matter how bleak the situation may seem to our natural eyes. The Lord is able to bring answers in ways that we can't even think or imagine. The Lord does the impossible on a daily basis and throughout Scripture we see how He delivered all those who kept steadfast in their faith. Another thing we must keep in mind is that the Lord brings peace to those who depend on Him. Ever since I accepted the Lord Jesus Christ as my Lord and Savior, God has been faithful to lead my life on to the best path and every need has been met. The Lord will be faithful to those who simply put their trust in Him. (Psalm 139:1-6) (Isaiah 55:8-9)

We must remember that God is faithful, God is trustworthy, God is loving and God is merciful. In Him is perfect peace that surpasses all understanding. He will perfect that which concerns us. If it is meant for our good, then it will be given to us so that our joy might be full. Be encouraged to trust and depend on the Lord all the days of your life. He will never leave you nor forsake you. The Lord is the strong tower that we can run to and have all our needs met. Trust Him and you will find yourself blessed beyond measure. (Philippians 4:4-7) (Isaiah 26:3)

Recognizing And Giving Praise To Others

We should always be quick to give praise to whom it is due. Many times we get so busy with our daily routines that we forget to recognize the efforts of those around us. We neglect to give an encouraging word, to praise a deed well done and to simply encourage those closest to us letting them know of how proud we are of them. It will not take a great effort on our part to lift them up, but to the recipient, it can mean the whole world. Sometimes people just need to be reminded that they are greatly loved and thought upon. When we go the extra step to reassure them with our love, that is when relationships are strengthened and a bond becomes unbreakable. (Galatians 6:8-10) (John 13:35)

Be encouraged to think on how you can speak a kind word, lift up and simply encourage and reassure that one who is near and dear to your heart. When we bless our relationships, that is good seed being planted in good ground. In due time the harvest will grow and we will see what great fruit will come forth from the seeds that were planted. Do your part today and be a blesser with your words. You will see what great impact your kind gestures will have upon others.

Brightening Our Path

It is important that we brighten the path that we walk upon so that it is illuminated for those who walk behind us and beside us. Brightening our path means that we do our absolute best to encourage those who are discouraged, to inspire those who are stagnant and unmoved and simply do our best to be a beacon of hope and love that people are drawn to and motivated to emulate. We who follow the example of the Lord Jesus Christ who condemned none and forgave and loved all should extend that same love towards our fellow man. (Galatians 6:9-10) (Matthew 5:13-16)

Let us take hold of the reins and be the initiators of good works. Let us love the unlovable, let us forgive the unforgivable and let us reconcile with those that have been distant from us. Mending relationships not only blesses the recipient, but our life becomes elevated as well. Being a world changer starts by impacting those closest to us first and then when they do the same for their neighbor, the ripple effects will continue on longer than we could ever think or imagine. (James 1:22-25) (1 Peter 4:8-11)

No matter what you may be going through and no matter how tough the trials in your path seem to be, I encourage you to be that beacon of hope, love, forgiveness and reconciliation. Let your life be the catalyst in which the lives of others are changed for the better forever. Use the gifts within your heart to draw all people back to the One who has given us the ability to be His ambassadors on this earth. (2 Corinthians 5:17-21) (Romans 12:15-21)

I wholeheartedly believe that a life well lived is a life lived in service to others. Let us be our brother's keeper and do all that we can to leave a long and lasting legacy of good works towards our fellow man.

That is a life that we can be proud to have lived.

Challenging Messages

The following messages are to challenge you to become better than we thought you can be, to forgive quicker than you had before, to love others unconditionally and to lead by example so that your life will shine brightly in the lives of those around you.

Doing The Right Thing At All Times

I have been thinking about the destruction of sin that comes to those who do not crucify their flesh and protect their mind from the wiles of the enemy's temptations and I felt the Lord leading me to write a message on this subject. I hope this message on resisting the enemy's temptations and protecting yourself from accepting his suggestions will minister to your heart and equip you to stand strong against his attacks and commit your heart anew to the Lord Jesus Christ.

The Bible declares in Galatians 6:7-8, "Be not deceived; God is not mocked: for whatsoever a man soweth, that shall he also reap. For he that soweth to his flesh shall of the flesh reap corruption; but he that soweth to the Spirit shall of the Spirit reap life everlasting." The Bible is very clear in its warning that when we sow only to the flesh that in the end we will reap corruption, but if we sow to the spirit we will reap the benefits of living righteously before the Lord. There are many temptations that come our way that subtly suggest to cheat a little, lie a little, steal a little and nobody will ever know. I want you to know that that is a lie straight from the pits of hell because the eyes of the Lord sees everything that is done openly and in secret. There is nothing that can be done without the Lord knowing about it. He is omniscient and omnipresent which means He sees all things at all times. (Psalm 139:1-6) (Matthew 6:1-8) (Psalm 139:7-13)

There is an excellent story in the Old Testament of temptation, greed, deceit and ultimately destruction that I would like to share with you. I will tell the main points of the story that is found in 2 Kings chapter 5. It is the story of Gehazi who was the servant of Elisha the Prophet. The story begins with a mighty warrior named Naaman who had leprosy and was in need of a healing. He heard of Elisha the Prophet and was sent word by the King of Aram that he was welcome to go to Israel to meet with Elisha and hopefully receive his healing. Naaman gathered his men and took with him silver, gold and expensive clothing hoping to give them to Elisha the man of God as gifts for his healing.

When Naaman arrived to the house of Elisha, Naaman was told by Elisha's messenger to go dip himself seven times in the Jordan River. Naaman was initially offended because he didn't believe by simply dipping himself in the river that he would be healed, but after his men urged him to follow Elisha's directions, he did so and was completely healed making his skin as smooth as a young child's. Naaman was so happy that he came before the Prophet Elijah offering him the silver, gold and garments as gifts of thanks, but Elisha refused them telling Naaman that he would not accept any gifts. Naaman accepted what Elisha had told him and after he had thanked Elisha again and praised the God of Israel, Naaman proceeded to return back to his home.

Now Gehazi who was Elisha's servant saw that Elisha didn't accept the gifts of Naaman and in his greed he thought that he could accept the gifts on behalf of Elisha without Elisha ever knowing about it. So Gehazi followed after Naaman and when he saw Gehazi running after him, Naaman got off his chariot to see what was the matter. Gehazi told him that he requested the silver and garments for two Prophets that had just arrived in town which was a lie. Naaman gladly gave him double of what he asked for and sent two men into town with Gehazi to carry the goods. Before they reached the town with the goods, Gehazi sent the men off and hid the goods in his house hoping that no one saw him.

When Gehazi entered the house of his master Elisha, Gehazi was asked where he had been. Gehazi answered Elisha and said he had not been anywhere. Elisha knew all that had taken place because of his prophetic gift and answered Gehazi as we read in 2 Kings 5:26-27 "But Elisha asked him, "Don't you realize that I was there in spirit when Naaman stepped down from his chariot to meet you? Is this the time to receive money and clothing and olive groves and vineyards and sheep and oxen and servants? Because you have done this, you and your children and your children's children will suffer from Naaman's leprosy forever." When Gehazi left the room, he was leprous; his skin was as white as snow." Gehazi not only lost his position as the servant of Elisha the Prophet, but was stricken with leprosy that would affect him and his descendants and is never mentioned in the Bible again.

The point that I want to emphasize is that sin can seem very appealing in the beginning and we believe the lie that no harm can come from our lying, cheating, stealing or whatever the sin may be, but that is not true because there is a Just God watching the actions that we do openly and in secret and He will reward us accordingly. Many people think of God as one who loves unconditionally and that is true, but He is also a Just God and a God of Judgment. Remember the scripture says God is not mocked and whatsoever a man sows that he will also reap. (1 Corinthians 6:9-11) (2 Thessalonians 1:5-8)

Be encouraged to do the right thing at all times not only when people are watching you, but also when no one is watching you because the Lord is a just Judge and will give to every person righteous judgment. Learn the lesson from Gehazi's story and do not fall for the enemy's tricks of greed and deceit, but rather live purely before the Lord asking Him to give you strength for each new day's trials. The Lord loves you and has made a way for you to escape every temptation, so you stand strong and know that with God by your side you can overcome every temptation of the enemy and come forth victorious. (2 Corinthians 5:9-11) (Psalm 18:29-33) (James 4:1-8)

Read and meditate on these scriptures:

James 1:13-17 "Let no man say when he is tempted, I am tempted of God: for God cannot be tempted with evil, neither tempteth He any man: But every man is tempted, when he is drawn away of his own lust, and enticed. Then when lust hath conceived, it bringeth forth sin: and sin, when it is finished, bringeth forth death. Do not err, my beloved brethren. Every good gift and every perfect gift is from above, and cometh down from the Father of lights, with whom is no variableness, neither shadow of turning."

2 Corinthians 10:3-5 "For though we walk in the flesh, we do not war after the flesh: (For the weapons of our warfare are not carnal, but mighty through God to the pulling down of strong holds;) Casting down imaginations and every high thing that exalteth itself against the knowledge of God, and bringing into captivity every thought to the obedience of Christ."

1 Corinthians 10:12-13 "Wherefore let him that thinketh he standeth take heed lest he fall. There hath no temptation taken you but such as is common to man: but God is faithful, who will not suffer you to be tempted above that ye are able; but will with the temptation also make a way to escape, that ye may be able to bear it."

All of these scriptures can be found in the King James Version Bible.

Believing In Ourselves Again

It is important in life that we believe in ourselves. It is important that we believe that we are meant for greatness and that our life can be used to make a great difference in this world. We must believe in ourselves because if we don't believe in ourselves then why should anyone else believe in us. Why should other people help us excel if we don't think we are deserving of it? Many times we get down on ourselves and we think that our life has no meaning or purpose. Having this type of mentality will keep our life stagnant, unproductive and unable to reach the heights of victory that were once so evident in our hearts and minds. No matter our past mistakes or shortfalls, we must believe that a second chance is available to us. We must believe that a new beginning is possible. When we make up our minds and be determined that our life is important and can be used to benefit humanity, that is when a positive change will begin to take place. (Ephesians 3:20) (Isaiah 43:18-19)

When we agree with God and allow His perfect will to take place in our life, that is when miracles will begin to happen for us. When times of discouragement come our way, we simply must remind ourselves that God does not create anything without a plan and purpose behind it. As long as we are alive on this Earth, then our story isn't finished yet. The fulfillment of our life hasn't reached its potential. Our life's work hasn't been fulfilled or accomplished. A new thing is always ahead of us. We simply must believe in ourselves and make ourselves available to reach those goals, desires and dreams that are waiting to be achieved and accomplished. It's okay to have a pity party for a short time, but we can't stay there. We can't allow our life to pass us by letting our dreams perish. (Ephesians 1:9) (1 John 5:14-15)

The saddest thing in life is unfulfilled dreams. There are so many people who die with their dream still inside of them. They didn't believe they were meant for greatness and they took their gifts, talents and dreams with them to their graves. Let's not let that happen to us. Let us not have any regrets in life. The things that we know we can do, we should not postpone for another day. Tomorrow is not promised to us, but we do have today to start on the journey to fulfill our life's purpose. Believe in yourself again and know that with God by your side all things are possible. Don't listen to the negative reports or those who choose to doubt your ability. Always remember that you and God are a majority. You don't need everyone in your corner; you just need the right One in your corner. When you do believe, that is when miracles take place. (Mark 9:23) (Mark 11:23-24)

Making Ourselves Available To Bless Others

There are so many opportunities in life where we can be a blessing to someone else in need. These opportunities don't always let us know when they're coming; they just present themselves in the moments when we're not expecting them. It is for this reason that we should always make ourselves available to be a blessing when we have the chance. However we may be used to bless someone else, we should do it. Someone may cross your path who is discouraged; you should use that opportunity to speak a blessing into their life. Let them know how special they are and how much they have to offer this world. You can complement the work they've done, the accomplishments they've achieved and let them know of the times that they have blessed you. (Galatians 6:10)

Many times people simply need to be reminded that goodness still exists in this world. There are so many people who are only interested in themselves and in what they're going through. They don't take the time to see the needs of others and that is not how God wishes for us to act. The Bible tells us to bear one another's burdens. We are to be our brother's keeper. We are to lift them up, encourage them, minister grace to them and let them know that we love them and more importantly that God loves them. (Galatians 6:2)

1 John 4:20-21 declares "If a man say, I love God, and hateth his brother, he is a liar: for he that loveth not his brother whom he hath seen, how can he love God whom he hath not seen? And this commandment have we from Him, That he who loveth God love his brother also." The Bible also declares in Colossians 3:12-14 "Therefore, as the elect of God, holy and dearly loved, clothe yourselves with a heart of mercy, kindness, humility, gentleness, and patience, bearing with one another and forgiving one another, if someone happens to have a complaint against anyone else. Just as the Lord has forgiven you, so you also forgive others."

Be encouraged to take the initiative to be a blessing in every opportunity that you have. Life is too short to spend it only wanting for our own well-being. We can't take the physical possessions with us when we die, but the things that we did to help, bless, encourage and lift up others will be shared forever in our hearts and in the hearts of those who received our kind acts. Think on the brevity of life and remember how short it is. We can use our time wisely to leave a mark that will never be forgotten or erased. Having that type of impact on humanity is a legacy that we can all be proud of.

Making An Extra Effort To Show Our Kindness

One thing that we can never do enough of or be forgotten for is our kindness. We can never be kind to too many people in life and the more kindness that we share with those around us, the more joy and happiness will be imparted into their lives. There are so many people in this world who are only interested in themselves and in what they are going through and they do not take the time to invest in the lives of others. They see kindness as unnecessary or something that "someone else" may be better at than themselves. What we must realize is that kindness, generosity and being selfless are all ways to show how much love we have in our hearts. (Romans 12:10)

We can say we love everyone to know end, but if we don't put in some effort behind it, then our words are all in vain. Just as the Bible says that faith without works is dead, so it is with love and kindness. These two must go together just as faith and works do. We have to show kindness to all people including those who have done us wrong in times past. The true measure of a man is not in how he treats his friends, but it is in how he treats those who have hurt him in times past. When we make an effort to show kindness, we will impart into the other person's life pure love that is without motive. That is how we can show all people the great love that God has placed within our hearts. (James 2:18-22) (Luke 6:32-36)

When we take the time to be encouraging, to give a simple gift, to listen to someone else's problems, to impart some wisdom into their life or to simply be a shoulder that they can lean upon, we are showing a kindness that will never be forgotten. They may forget many things about you, but they will never forget how you made them feel. When we speak to someone's heart, that is an impartation that is eternal. I encourage you to see the benefits of showing kindness to those around you. It may be your family, your friends, your co-workers or complete strangers. It does not matter who you are kind to, what does matter is that you make an effort to be kind in any situation and show the love that emanates from your being.

Life is too short to spend it in hatred, in backbiting and in gossip. Let us break from any past animosities and do our best to act as Christ's ambassadors on this Earth and be loving, kind and tenderhearted towards everyone we come into contact with. Leaving that type of legacy will keep your memory alive in the hearts of everyone you have touched.

Staying Faithful To God

I have been thinking about the faithfulness of God's servants throughout the Bible and I felt the Lord leading me to write a message on what would have happened if a couple of God's servants chose to quit their task because they were discouraged or felt unfit to accomplish the task that God had placed on their hearts. I hope you are encouraged and inspired by this message to never give up on the task that God has placed on your heart.

I think about the faithfulness of the Apostle Paul. What if one day the Apostle Paul who was sitting in jail decided that he had suffered enough for the sake of the Gospel and chose not to write any of the great epistles which would eventually become a big part of the New Testament? If the Apostle Paul quit the task that God placed in his heart, we would not have such great, inspiring and powerful scriptures such as, "I can do all things through Christ", "If God be for us, who can be against us?", "Be strong in the Lord and in the power of His might". The Apostle Paul was encouraging the saints to move forward and be strong even while he himself was both chained and in a prison. (Philippians 4:13) (Romans 8:31) (Ephesians 6:10)

I think about Noah's faithfulness. What if after building the arc for 80 years Noah got discouraged and quit building the arc because there were no signs of rain and everyone around Noah was mocking his efforts? All of the Earth's creatures as well as Noah and his family would not

143

have been saved from the flood. There would not have been a chance for mankind to replenish the earth both through the animals as well as the rebirth of the entire human population. Because Noah stayed faithful, there are now over 7 billion people alive on this Earth. (Genesis 7:17-24) (Genesis 9:1-7)

We must understand that both Noah and the Apostle Paul were human just as we are and they felt the same emotions that we feel today and yet each continued in and fulfilled God's plan for their life. The point I want to make is that no matter how frustrated you may get or how discouraged you may feel because of the trials of life, you mustn't ever quit the task that God has placed on your heart. You may not see any fruit right now and think that your time and effort is all in vain, but I can assure you that someone will benefit and receive great blessings because of your unfailing determination. (Hebrews 11:7) (Ephesians 3:13) (Hebrews 12:2-3)

I encourage you to never allow the voice of discouragement to enter your heart. Stay steadfast and determined in accomplishing every goal that God has placed in your heart. The Bible says to be strong in the Lord and in the power of His might. We cannot be strong in our own might or ability, but we can be strong in the Lord. Take comfort in the Lord's promise and know that great things will come forth because of your steadfast faith and determination in reaching every goal that is in your heart. (Ephesians 6:10-14)

Read and meditate on these scriptures:

Psalm 37:1-5 "Fret not thyself because of evildoers, neither be thou envious against the workers of iniquity. For they shall soon be cut down like the grass, and wither as the green herb. Trust in the LORD, and do good; so shalt thou dwell in the land, and verily thou shalt be fed. Delight thyself also in the LORD; and He shall give thee the desires of thine heart. Commit thy way unto the LORD; trust also in Him; and He shall bring it to pass."

Philippians 3:13-14 "Brethren, I count not myself to have apprehended: but this one thing I do, forgetting those things which are behind, and reaching forth unto those things which are before, I press toward the mark for the prize of the high calling of God in Christ Jesus."

Hebrews 12:1-3 "Wherefore seeing we also are compassed about with so great a cloud of witnesses, let us lay aside every weight, and the sin which doth so easily beset us, and let us run with patience the race that is set before us, Looking unto Jesus the author and finisher of our faith; who for the joy that was set before Him endured the cross, despising the shame, and is set down at the right hand of the throne of God. For consider Him that endured such contradiction of sinners against Himself, lest ye be wearied and faint in your minds."

All scriptures can be found in the King James Version Bible.

Making Our Love Known

We should always be quick to recognize what is most important in life. Many times we become so busy with our daily routines that we forget to take the time to spend with those who mean the most to us. When we place schedules and routines above our relationships, in time those relationships will fracture because they are not receiving the attention that they deserve. Anything that is neglected will eventually perish. When we don't nurture the relationships that we have with our spouse, children, parents, siblings and friends then we will lose the connection that we have with them. They will feel unimportant and believe that we don't care about their feelings or what they're going through in life. (1 Corinthians 3:8-10)

Just because we may be busy is no reason to neglect or forget those who mean the world to us. Feeling a certain way towards someone and showing them how you feel are two different things. You may love your spouse, children, family, etc. to know end, but if you don't tell them and show them with your words and actions, then they will never truly know. Words not spoken are often times words not felt. We have to make an effort in our relationships. It may be something simple or something that may take a little extra time, but effort must be put in so that our relationships can continue to grow and flourish for the rest of our life. (Hebrews 10:24-25) (1 John 4:7)

Be encouraged to think on how you're spending your time. Are you investing wisely in the lives of those closest to you? Are you listening to their stories, concerns and worries? Are you encouraging them, inspiring them, challenging them and showing them how special they are and how much they have to offer this world? We are a big influence whether we realize it or not and our attention or lack thereof will have a great impact upon those whom we love. Be encouraged to take the initiative and see how important spending time with your loved ones really is. Nurture your relationships; let your love be made known. Do something special for them for no particular reason and reiterate to them how much you love them and how much they mean to you. Do not allow another day to pass you by without showing your love. All that we will have in the end is the love that we purposefully gave out to those who meant the world to us. (1 John 4:1013)

Believing That You Are Meant For More

We should always strive to become better in life. We should never become accustomed to a situation when we know in our hearts that we are meant for more. Striving for excellence, reaching for greater heights, having a deep hunger to better ourselves are proven ways to reach the goals and desires that are deep within our hearts. Many times we feel like giving up on our dreams and we stop pursuing the goals that were once so evident in our hearts because of the trials and tribulations of life. We become discouraged because of our financial situation, our failing health, our family obligations, etc. We place our betterment on hold because we believe the lie that this is our lot in life and that more is not meant for us. What we must remind ourselves is that God is able to help us reach greater heights than we can even think or imagine, but we have to take the initiative and start trying to reach them. We have to believe in ourselves again just as God believes in us and do the things that are necessary to bring our dreams into reality. If that means studying more, exercising more, working more, sacrificing more or practicing more, then we should do it with all diligence. We can't expect results to simply fall into our laps. Hard work is necessary in any endeavor to reach excellence. (Psalm 34:4-10) (Psalm 37:4-5)

We will be successful when we are diligent. A popular quote says "The early bird catches the worm." In other words, we have to work hard in order to realize our dreams. We may have to get up early and stay up late, but if we stick with it, in time progress will come and our dreams will be realized. I encourage you to believe in yourself. Don't let your years go by without trying your best in life. Do not settle for mediocrity, but reach for the greatest heights possible. The Lord who has created us has instilled greatness within our being, but it is up to us to reach for greatness. We have to believe for ourselves before any results are seen.

If you are finding yourself stuck, I encourage you to seek the Lord in prayer and ask for His guidance to lead you to your next level. The Lord is able to do exceeding abundantly above all that we can ask or even think. Believe Him and strive to reach every desire that is within your heart. (Psalm 147:11) (Ephesians 3:20-21)

Mastering Our Time Wisely

There are many moments in life when we waste the precious time that we have been given on things that have no importance or relevance towards our future. What we must realize is that time passes by so quickly and without seeing it in those moments, we can testify that years have gone by that had no significance in making our life better than it was before. Things that we should have done were postponed for later dates when we "had more time" to do those things. Now that we look back, we regret not taking the initiative and fulfilling the desires that were so evident in our hearts before. The good news is that we still have the opportunity while we are alive on this Earth to do the things that will have significance where time is concerned. (Psalm 31:14-15) (2 Peter 1:5-10)

We can help to better our family, we can be encouraging and inspirational to our friends and acquaintances, we can take that trip that has been postponed numerous times, we can spend time alone with God in prayer thanking Him for all that He has given us throughout our lifetime. Knowing that time passes by so quickly should make us stop and reevaluate how we are spending it. Are we doing the things that make a difference? Are we benefiting from our time? Are we using our time wisely? Answering these questions is very simple, but doing something about it is where we find it difficult. (1 Thessalonians 5:18)

We make excuses of why we can't do certain things with our time i.e., our kids, our jobs, our health constraints, our financial constraints, etc. If we look past these excuses and make our mind up to use our time as best as we can, we will live life to its fullest potential. We will become masters of our time instead of time being our master. Be encouraged to see how you could spend your time better. Focus on the important things and see where changes need to be made and make them. Do not postpone. Let us not have regrets when we enter into Eternity. Let us fulfill our life's mission now while we have the opportunity to do so. By appreciating and managing your time better, you will have lived a fulfilled life.

Seeing The True Beauty Of Others

There are many instances in life where we put a great emphasis on physical beauty. We judge ourselves and others based upon how we look instead of looking deeper within someone's heart and judging them based on their character and personality. What we must remember is that beauty does not define a person. I've met many "beautiful" people in my life and some of them were the "ugliest" people on the inside that I had ever met. Looks will not impress for long because beauty fades, but the depth of love, care and compassion that comes from one's heart is beauty that lasts forever. No matter how one looks physically, if they are beautiful on the inside than that beauty will shine all the way through to their exterior as well. (1 Samuel 16:7)

We should never dismiss someone simply because they don't look a certain way. It doesn't matter if they're tall, short, skinny or heavyset. It doesn't matter if they're light skinned or dark skinned. It doesn't matter if their eyes are blue, green, brown or black. It doesn't matter if their nose is too big or too small, if they're big chinned or no chinned. Someone's physical appearance doesn't necessarily mean that they are more than or less than any other person and if we judge others based solely on their beauty or lack thereof, we will be missing out on some pretty spectacular relationships so let us look deeper within one's heart and see their true beauty. Let us not be vain and superficial only focusing on the surface. By focusing deeper into one's heart, we will see a lasting beauty and we will build a lasting relationship. (Luke 6:37) (John 7:24)

Be encouraged to take this message to heart and re-examine how you interact with others. You may be missing out on a special friendship or relationship because you have dismissed someone in times past because they didn't look a certain way or they didn't have your "preference". I encourage you again to be more open to others and allow special friendships to be formed. You will be enriching your own life in ways that you can't imagine and you will build relationships that will last a lifetime. You will be proud of yourself for looking deeper into one's heart and seeing their true and lasting beauty.

Having The Right Attitude

When times of testing come our way and we are tempted to murmur and complain, we should pause a moment and think on how God has intervened in times past and brought resolution. Instead of complaining to the Lord, we should thank Him for never leaving our side in times past and remember the lessons that were learned. We gain so much when we go through the difficult times. We learn perseverance, we develop character and our resolve is strengthened. We don't notice these betterments until after the trial has been overcome, but by knowing now that we'll come forth stronger after the challenge or trial, then we should face it with faith, joy and expectancy that we will be better in the end because of it. (Philippians 2:14-15) (James 1:2-4)

When we recognize that problems serve a purpose, we will no longer be discouraged when problems come our way, but rather we will see it as a means in becoming better, wiser and stronger than we were before that situation. Our attitude determines the heights we will reach, but it also determines our lows. How we see a situation is dependent on our attitude and outlook. We should always trust the Lord and be optimistic in the midst of the trials. We are to see the glass as half-full and never half empty. We are to praise the Lord and give thanks that He has not left our side and that our victory is surely ahead of us. Faith must be aimed in the right direction. Our faith can work for us or it can work against us. Again, it is dependent on our attitude. (Proverbs 27:17) (Philippians 4:11-13)

The words that we speak must be faith filled and not doubt ridden. We can't expect victory by speaking defeat. Our words must line up with the Word of God and our actions must be in tune with our words. Our words have creative power. Our words bring into existence what we continually say and that is why we should be careful to only speak encouraging, overcoming, faith filled words. Be encouraged to have a cheerful countenance. See your many blessings and do not focus on the hardships before you. By being determined to praise God in the midst of our struggles, we are ensuring our victory. The Lord loves to show Himself strong on behalf of those who trust Him. Let us show God that we are determined to have the victory.

Leading By Example

In this day that we're living, people need to see more than ever that goodness still exists in one another. People are so jaded these days because they have been hurt numerous times by numerous people. Everyone has their guard up, everyone questions the motives of others and even when someone takes the initiative to do a kind deed, it is sometimes received with hesitation. I believe it is because many people don't give with a pure heart. They give with motives, with intentions behind the gift and not because it is done in love. What we must realize is that all we have to offer is love. When we give without motive, without pretense, without wanting in return, we will be known for our love. We will become in essence attractive because others will know that our heart is pure and full of love just as the Lord is towards His creation. (Galatians 6:9-10) (Matthew 6:1-4)

The Lord is our example and just as He loved, forgave, encouraged and ministered to those in need, so must we follow in His footsteps. When we act as Christ did, we will be recognized as His disciples, His followers, His workmen. A legacy that we can be proud of is when others recognize us by our good works, by our love, by our compassion. That is what I want to be remembered for and I pray that same motivation will be upon you for the rest of your life. (Luke 6:36)

Loving Our Neighbor

There are many Bible believing Christians in this world that want to make a great impact on society and their earnest prayers are to be used of God in magnificent and extraordinary ways. What we must always keep in mind is that God does not call every believer to be an Evangelist or Missionary to travel the world, but He does call every believer to love their neighbor as themselves. The way that we can reach the world with the saving and healing message of Jesus Christ is for each of us to care for and take interest in those around us who are in need. (John 1:10-12) (Mark 12:30-31)

Imagine the impact on this world if every believer looks to their left and to their right and made a conscious decision to reach those people who are so near with the life changing message that Jesus Christ loves them and died and rose again so that they may Live Eternally. (Ezekiel 36:25-27)

Leaving A Lasting Legacy

There are many people in this world who go about living their life without giving much attention to their legacy. They don't think about how they will be remembered. They don't focus on what they did to help make someone else's life a little bit better. One thing we must always think about is our legacy. What did we do with our life that helped someone else excel in their life? What will we be remembered for long after we are gone? Will we be remembered for our selfishness or for our selflessness? Will we be thought about with fondness and talked about with future generations or will our life's memory quickly pass from their minds? (Proverbs 22:1) (Ecclesiastes 7:1)

These are important questions that we should ask ourselves so that we can evaluate how useful our life really is. It will not matter how big our bank account is when we die or how many accomplishments we were able to attain. What will matter is what we did to help our family and friends reach higher, become better and show them that they can excel in any area that they are lacking. When we make our life one of service everyone will benefit. We will be blessed for having the opportunity to bless others and the recipient will be blessed because they were able to become better than they were before. (1 Peter 3:10-12)

We must always remember and keep in mind that those who receive our help will remember it far longer than we ever will. Never believe the lie that you should only want for yourself and for your own well-being. Looking out for others is what catapults our life to greater heights. When we help others excel, our life is made richer. When we offer forgiveness, encouragement and inspiration, their life is lifted up and shown that a new beginning is possible no matter their past mistakes or shortfalls. We are rekindling the flame in their spirit and showing them by our example that it's never the end of the story until you have exhaled your last breath. Be encouraged to leave a lasting legacy of love, forgiveness, encouragement, inspiration and motivation. Make it a goal to leave a blessed legacy. Leave footprints that no one else can forget so that when you are thought upon, a lasting smile will be upon the faces of those whom you were blessed enough to touch. (Philippians 2:2-3)

Forgetting The Past And Looking Forward To A Better Future

There are many times that we get down on ourselves for the mistakes that we've made in our past and instead of learning the lesson and becoming better because of it, we become depressed, discouraged and think our future is without hope. What we must realize and recognize is that a new beginning is always available with the Lord. We may fall short a thousand times, but His mercy and grace will be there to lift us up each and every time and that still small voice will encourage us to try better next time. We should never think our best days are behind us. As long as we have breath in our lungs, then our story isn't finished yet. We still have opportunities to do better, reach higher and accomplish the goals that we had given up on. No matter our past, we can begin again. The problem lies in forgetting and forgiving ourselves for the many times that we failed. It is in getting past our past that we can begin to look towards our future. We can't walk forward looking backwards. Our past mistakes must stay there and we must strive to look forward, to do better and to reach higher than we've ever believed we could before. (Philippians 3:13-14) (Isaiah 43:19)

If you have been stuck in a rut of unforgiveness and stagnation thinking that nothing good will ever come your way again, I want you to know that a new beginning is possible. You simply must stand up, dust yourself off and ask the Lord to give you the strength and ability to do better than you've ever done before. It is in our hands how our days go. We can murmur and complain about all the difficulties we've faced or we can be thankful that the difficulties helped to teach us lessons that we could not have learned otherwise. The problems, trials, heartaches all serve a purpose to make us wiser, stronger and better than we were before. We simply must accept each difficulty as a lesson learned and use it to our benefit now in our present and in our future to come. Be encouraged to let your past stay there. Don't look back on it, don't think about it and don't give it any attention. Use that energy to focus ahead. We can't drive forward with our eyes on the rearview mirror because inevitably we will crash. Keeping our eyes focused on our future, praying for strength and being determined that we will do better this time is what will cause us to have success in every area of our life. Believe it for yourself and strive to achieve it each day that you have. (Romans 8:34) (Isaiah 1:18)

The Power of Our Words

We should never underestimate the power of our kind words. Whether we realize it or not the things we say to others does resonate in their hearts and can encourage them to see how valuable they are and how much they have to offer. Many times people face difficulties that seem overwhelming and they believe the lie that they can't overcome for one reason or another. That is all the more reason that we should invest in their lives with our positive and affirming words reminding them of their unique abilities, gifts and talents that no one else possesses. Just as we sometimes forget how special we are, we should remember to remind others of how special they are. We are to lift one another up in the difficult times, bearing one another's burdens and simply be there to show that we care for their well-being. True love as God wishes for us to have is to love our neighbor as ourselves without motive, without pretense and without judgment. (Proverbs 18:21) (Romans 14:19) (1 Thessalonians 5:11)

Be encouraged to take the initiative to say a kind word to those around you. Notice something that they do well and compliment them on it. Be sensitive in your judgment. Don't criticize too harshly. Our words penetrate deeply whether in giving compliments or in giving criticism. Those in need of our praise may have already suffered greatly by the hands of others and they don't need our condemnation as well. As Christ's ambassadors let us lift up, encourage, strengthen and motivate all those whom we are lucky enough to cross paths with. Let us leave a legacy of blessing in the lives of others so that their life may reach its full potential. We can live on forever in the hearts of those whom we have helped to make better. Let us strive to change lives for the better each day that God has given us on this Earth. That is my prayer. (1 John 3:17-18)

Recognizing Our Love Of Family

The personal relationships that we have with our loved ones are a gift that should be cherished and thought upon throughout our life. We have been given gifts that are meant to enrich us, strengthen us, encourage us, lift us up, and simply be there for us and these gifts are called our family. They are the ones who love us most and no matter what happens, they are the ones who will be there for us in good times and in bad. That is why we should be thankful for our family and do all that we can to let them know of our appreciation and help to make their life just a little bit better. Being there for one another is what strengthens our relationships and proves to be the solid bond that holds us together for generations. (1 John 4:20-21)

Be encouraged to be thankful for your loved ones and make known to them how much they mean to you. Making our love known is much more valuable to them than just keeping it to ourselves. We may love someone to know end, but if we don't tell them how we feel, then it is a missed opportunity to brighten their day and encourage them with our love. Seize every opportunity that you have to spend time with your family because in the end they are the ones who will mean the most to us. (1 John 4:7-8)

Sowing Goodness In People's Lives

We should always be quick to bless others when we have the opportunity. I've learned the secret to a blessed life and it has much to do with how giving our hearts are. The blessed person is the one who gives without motive, loves without pretense, listens without judgment and lifts up those who are downtrodden. We must remember that blessing others is how we get blessed, giving to others is how we gain the most and loving others is what fills our heart with the most love. It all goes back to sowing and reaping. Whatever we put into the ground is what will grow and come back to us one day. Whether we are sowing goodness and mercy or hatred and strife, we should expect to receive the same in abundance. We shouldn't be surprised when bad things return to us when the seeds we planted called for that harvest. (Galatians 6:10) (Luke 6:31)

We should always remember the frailty of life and the short time that we've been given on the Earth to live productively. How do we live productively? We do that by sowing goodness, mercy, love, encouragement. We bless others by leaving a situation better than when we found it. Life is too short to live it with regrets. That is why we should use our life to make a difference that can never be erased. Leaving a mark for good so that our legacy will live on long after our time has ended is what each of us should strive to do. Be encouraged to make your legacy one that will live on forever. Let your good works speak on your behalf because in doing so you will be exalting the name of the Lord on whose behalf every good work was done. Praise God. That is my wish for my life and the lives of those I am blessed enough to be in contact with. (Galatians 6:7-8)

Having The Right Attitude

It is important that we always have the right attitude in life. There are many moments when we are tempted to lose our peace and murmur and complain about all that is going wrong in our life. It is in these moments that we must be conscious to how we react to circumstances that are trying to steal our peace. We must be steadfast and vigilant determined to react in the correct manner and allow ourselves to stay at peace regardless of the wrong that is going on around us. Our attitude should be one filled with gratitude, gratefulness, appreciation, humility and an eagerness to see the good that tomorrow holds. Just because we are facing tough times today does not mean our attitude should reflect those difficulties. Our countenance can remain steadfast to show our peacefulness no matter the storms that are raging around us. We can keep our faith strong in the Lord knowing that if He has brought us to the trial, then He will also bring us through the trial better than we were before it. We simply must maintain an attitude of praise in the midst of the trial and show God that our eyes of faith are focused on Him. (Isaiah 26:3-4) (Psalm 11:7)

Be encouraged to realize how important having the right attitude is. It is easy to murmur and complain when tough times come our way, but I believe it takes a real strong person to maintain their integrity, their character, their faith and their trust in the Lord that all will turn out well.

An attitude of appreciation and expectancy for good is what will turn a bad situation into one of being a lesson learned and being made better because of it. We can either see our glass half-full or half-empty. It all depends on our attitude. We can be appreciative and thankful that we will overcome the trial before us, or we can murmur and complain about how tired we are from going through the storm. The right attitude will make the best from a bad situation. It will see the sun coming through even in the midst of a cloud filled sky. The right attitude will have expectancy that good will come our way no matter how bad our situation may look right now. Be encouraged to adopt a positive, upbeat and faith filled attitude. It will make your burden much lighter and your path much clearer. (Psalm 121:5-8) (Psalm 34:8-9)

Living Life To The Full

With the unpredictability of life, we should always do our best in every area of life whether it be in our personal relationships, professional work environment, dealing with strangers and even completing certain tasks. We should do our work with excellence and a deep knowing in our hearts that we did our absolute best. Life is too short to live it with regrets and when we do something halfheartedly then we are not giving ourselves or others the chance to get the best of what we have to offer. That is why I believe giving our all in any particular task whether it be personal or professional is so important. We will not have a second chance to make a first impression. We won't be able to revisit a task after it has been completed and when we don't do it at our best the first time with all of our attention, with all of our zeal, with all of our wisdom and knowledge, then we are not giving our absolute best and that is where we fail. We may not realize in that moment, but when we think back on it over time, that is when regret will come into the picture. (Colossians 3:22-24) (Philippians 2:14-16)

Realizing that regrets can do so much to ruin otherwise beautiful memories, we should live in the moment more and have our mind future conscious so that when that memory does reach the future, we will have already realized we did our best back when we were in the moment. Regrets fill the minds and hearts of so many people because they didn't realize or acknowledge the fact that they could have done better in the past. Living future conscious makes our acts and deeds more calculated and careful and that is so important in living life to the fullest. Doing our best, loving with a pure heart, giving without motive, teaching to help others rise higher and forgiving for our own betterment is what each of us should strive to do each and every day that we are alive. Living a full life is all that we can ask of ourselves and that's what we should do each new day that we are lucky enough to see. (Mark 11:24-26) (Luke 6:35-38)

Being Joyful In The Midst Of Adversity

We all have many things to be joyful about in life, but many times we allow the temporary trials and setbacks to make us forget how blessed we truly are. It is in focusing on the good in the midst of the trial that we find how much we still have to be thankful for. If we only murmur and complain about all the bad that is happening to us and around us, it is human nature to want to have a pity party and feel sorry for ourselves, but if we change our mentality and choose to focus on the abundance that we have, the pity party will not last long. We will be consciously acknowledging that God is in control of all things and if He has brought a trial into our life, it is there to serve a purpose in making us stronger, wiser and better than we were before. We will learn the lesson, grow from it and move on to greater heights that God has prepared. Doing this without murmuring or questioning pleases God and frustrates the enemy to no end. (Psalm 103:1-5) (Psalm 111:1-5) (Psalm 46:1-5)

When Job had everything taken away from him, his wife told him to curse God and die. Job answered her in a profound way and I believe we should take on the same mentality. We read in Job 2:9-10 "Then his wife said to him, "Do you still hold fast to your integrity? Curse God and die!" But he said to her, "You speak as one of the foolish women speaks. Shall we indeed accept good from God, and shall we not accept adversity?" In all this Job did not sin with his lips." We can learn a lesson from Job that good and bad are promised to come our way, but our countenance should not be changed based on which one is present in our life.

We should be steadfast in faith knowing that God loves us and will meet our needs. We simply must remain confident in Him and know that all things will work together for our good. At the end of Job's trial, God gave him double of everything he had before. Be encouraged to keep your joyfulness no matter what may come and in the midst of your trial dare to give God thanks and praise that All Is Well. (John 16:33)

Loving Your Life Right Now

It is easy to become frustrated and even discouraged when we look at what others possess and wonder why we don't have the same things in our life. Whether it be marriage, children, finances or material possessions, it is easy to look at the lives of others and wonder "why not me?" What we must realize is that every person is created uniquely by the Hands of Almighty God and just as each of us differs in our creation, so too are His plans different for each of our lives. Each of us have a divine destiny that is meant to be fulfilled, but if we play the blame game with God and murmur and complain about how miserable life is, then our life will never reach its divine fulfillment because we will have fallen off our path and wished for the path of another. Instead of blazing our own trail, we will have wished to follow the trail that others have paved which isn't meant for us. (Proverbs 14:30) (Romans 13:13-14) (Galatians 5:22-26)

We must realize and recognize our uniqueness and know that God's plan for our life is perfect on its own. When we surrender our will and ask for God's will to be done, divine peace will fill our hearts and we will have a deep knowing in our spirit that we are on the right path. Be encouraged to trust God with your life and seek Him in prayer if you find yourself questioning His plans. The Lord is able to comfort your heart and give you peace that surpasses all understanding. We simply must seek Him and ask for the answers to be made clear in our hearts. Then we will know that our life is just as blessed as the next person whom we had thought had the ideal life. (Philippians 2:2-9)

Allowing Forgiveness To Take Root

We should always have a forgiving heart because holding on to grudges does nothing to heal the hurt or bring peace to your mind and soul. When we forgive others for their shortfalls against us, we are not condoning what they did, but we are showing Christ's centeredness in our lives and that just as we have been forgiven for our great sins, we must also forgive those who do wrong against us. We forgive not because we are weak, but because the Lord who is strong in us commands that we forgive those who have done wrong to us. Another thing that we must keep in mind is that forgiveness is more beneficial to us than to the ones we forgive. When we forgive, we release ourselves from the bondage of hate and open ourselves to receive the love, joy and peace that God wishes to infiltrate our heart with. (Matthew 6:14-15) (Matthew 5:7-10)

The Lord wishes to bring healing to our hearts, but we must take the first step to forgive the wrong that was done to us so that healing can begin. Be encouraged to see the benefits of having a forgiving heart. No matter what was done to you, the Lord is able to make you forget and not bring into remembrance. The only thing that you are required to do is to see past the hurt and allow forgiveness. When we do, great things will begin to take place in our life.

Message On Character And Integrity

It is important that we always keep integrity at the center of our lives. No matter the issue whether it be personal or professional, we should always be honest in our motives and pure hearted in our dealings. Life is too short to ruin our reputation for short term gain, but many times people don't see the big picture and quickly compromise their character and integrity for monetary gain or for pompous egotism. They want to be seen as important or highly regarded and portray themselves in a false light hoping their lies never see the light of day. What those people don't realize is that the truth lives on forever and leading their life in a false manner will backfire on them one day and everything that was hidden, untrue and made secret will come to light one day. When people's lies are brought to the forefront, nothing but shame, dishonor and heartache come from it. The results of all their misdealings would not have been worth it in the end because all that they gained from their deceit will be lost and more importantly their name will be irreparable. (Psalm 25:20-21) (Proverbs 11:3-5)

This is why I believe we should always lead our life in truth, honesty and integrity. Doing that which is right no matter who is watching is what pleases the Lord and leads our life onto the best path. Doing right when no one else is looking is what each of us should continually strive to do. No matter the temptation, always see integrity as most important. Know that it will save you when you need it most and it will guard your life when you least expect it. Be encouraged to live your life with integrity and know that when you do your name will live on forever. (Proverbs 19:1) (Numbers 32:23)

Focusing On The Right Things

We should always have a friendly countenance and demeanor about ourselves and remember that as children of the Lord, we should be quick to be kind, compassionate and loving towards everyone we come into contact with. Many times we see someone and know right away that they're having a hard time and need to be encouraged. We should take the initiative to be their "Angel" in that moment to lift them up, encourage them and show them how much life has to offer. We must remember that it is in looking at our blessings that we become encouraged and shown how privileged and favored we truly are. (Psalm 16:8-11) (Psalm 1:1-3)

Many times people simply need to be shown and reminded that goodness still exists within humanity and life no matter how difficult it may sometimes get can be enjoyed if we focus on the right things. We need to see how abundantly blessed we truly are and when we do, gratitude, thanksgiving and a cheerful heart will fill our being. Be encouraged to share joy whenever you see the opportunity and do all that you can to make a bad situation a little bit better. (1 John 2:9-11)

Returning Good For Evil

The Light that God has instilled in our hearts is meant to shine forth to brighten a dark and lonely world. We must always remember that we are ambassadors for Christ and as such we are to be the shining example of His love, care and forgiveness. When others treat us harshly and do not share simple consideration, we are not to take it personally, but rather see it as an opportunity to return good instead of evil. Jesus said it this way in Matthew 5:38-39 "You have heard that it was said, 'An eye for an eye and a tooth for a tooth.' But I tell you not to resist an evil person. But whoever slaps you on your right cheek, turn the other to him also."

We have received mercy and forgiveness from the Lord for our transgressions and as forgiven recipients we are to share that same mercy and forgiveness towards those who have done something wrong against us. We are to let our light shine brightly in the midst of darkness where all who see us will know Whom we belong to. (Matthew 5:16) (2 Cor. 5:18-21) (Romans 12:14-21)

Edifying Messages

The word edify is defined as to instruct and improve spiritually. That is what the following messages are meant to do. I pray that you will receive from each of the following messages the edification that they were purposed for.

Letting The Lord Lead Our Life

We should always allow the Lord to lead and guide us onto the best path for our life. There are so many instances when we want to do things our way and we don't consult the Lord first. We do things our way because we think we have all the answers and if we're being honest with ourselves, we know that we do not. We don't have all the answers because we don't know what our future holds. We don't know what surprises will be coming a week, a month or a year from now. The best thing that we can do is to ask the Lord to help us on our journey and guide us onto the best path as He sees fit. Why should we consult the Lord? We should consult the Lord because He knows all things in all places at all times. The Lord is omniscient, omnipotent and omnipresent. There is nothing that can surprise God or catch Him off guard. The Lord is able to bring answers in ways that we have never even thought of or imagined. He is the perfect guide for our lives because He loves us with an unending, unwavering and unfailing love. Just as a father loves his child and wishes for them to be blessed in their life, so the Lord wishes for us to be blessed, joyful, encouraged, inspired, filled with hope and have a deep knowing beyond any shadow of a doubt that our Heavenly Father loves us and He will never leave us nor forsake us. His love is without motive. It is pure and everlasting. Having that type of love should make us run to the Lord when we need guidance for our life. (Isaiah 30:21) (Deuteronomy 5:32-33)

Some might ask what should we seek guidance for? We should seek guidance for the things that we don't have the answers to. If we are seeking employment for instance, we should ask the Lord to lead us to the best job possible. We should ask for wisdom and understanding, we should ask for supernatural favor and we should praise God in the midst of our requests letting Him know that we trust that the best outcome is coming our way. Prayer and praise need to go hand in hand because that is showing God our dependence on Him in our prayers and our praise shows God that we are thankful that He hears us and that the answer is on the way. By having confidence in the Lord we are blessing our own future. We are signifying through our confidence that all will be well. No matter how dark the situation may seem and no matter how hard the storm is raging around us, when we have confidence in the Lord in the midst of our setbacks, we are boldly declaring that God is by our side and nothing shall be able to take us out of His Hands. (Isaiah 26:3-4) (Colossians 3:14-15) (Psalm 118:8-9)

Be encouraged to see your need for the Lord's guidance and direction in your life. You may think you have all the answers, but I assure you that you do not. There will come a time in your life when you will need direction. There will come a time when you don't know what to do. Don't wait for that time to call upon the Lord. Call upon Him now and with your prayer and praise let all of your requests be made known to God. The Bible says when we make our requests known unto Him, the peace of God shall rule in our hearts and He will keep us in perfect peace. Perfect peace is worth more than all of the riches of this world. You don't need to have the physical possessions to be at peace. No matter where you are right now, the Lord can give you that peace. You simply must seek Him and when you do, the Lord will be faithful to answer. Always remember that God loves you and wishes for you to prosper and be in health even as your soul prospers. (Philippians 4:6-7) (3 John 2)

The Power of The Seed

I have been thinking about the power of the seed and the Lord has been speaking to my heart to write a message on this subject. I believe the seed when understood correctly can greatly improve people's lives and show them that many of our blessings and our cursings come from the seeds that we've sown. I hope this message shows you the importance of sowing seed correctly and the great benefits that come from understanding the seed.

One thing we should understand is that we sow seeds every day either in our own lives or in the lives of others. We sow seeds physically, emotionally, spiritually and mentally. Every seed that we sow brings its own harvest either for good or for bad. When we do something kind for others such as giving them a gift, we are sowing seeds of blessings and joy. When we say a kind word, we are sowing seeds of love and affirmation. When we pray for others and ask God to meet their need or help them in an area that they are struggling, we are sowing seeds of hope, mercy and grace. When we acknowledge a deed well done or compliment someone on a talent they possess, we are sowing seeds of encouragement.

Every seed that we sow will fall into the soil of someone's heart. It will take root, grow and bring to fruition what was planted by us the sower. That is why we must be conscious to what we are saying and doing to others. We are either planting good seeds to bless, encourage and strengthen them or we are planting bad seeds that will discourage others and make them doubt their true greatness. Let us remember the power of our actions and be diligent in lifting others up and showing them the true greatness that lies within their being.

Another area concerning the seed is giving to God financially. How do we give to God? In the Old Testament all people were commanded to give a tenth of what they had back to God and that would ensure their continued blessing from Him. As New Testament Christians, we are not commanded to give 10% of our income, but we are told to give as much as comes from our heart. We read in 2 Corinthians 9:7-8 "Every man according as he purposeth in his heart, so let him give; not grudgingly, or of necessity: for God loveth a cheerful giver. And God is able to make all grace abound toward you; that ye, always having all sufficiency in all things, may abound to every good work." We are told to give cheerfully and because we do, God will make His grace abound towards us.

Just as seeds take root in the soil and grow and brings its own harvest, so it is with those who give financially to God. The Lord is able to multiply the seed given and return it back to the giver. The Lord Jesus declares in Luke 6:38 "Give, and it shall be given unto you; good measure, pressed down, and shaken together, and running over, shall men give into your bosom. For with the same measure that ye mete withal it shall be measured to you again." If we place our money in banks and we receive the small interest that we do, then how much more will God multiply our seed for being obedient to His Word and giving cheerfully from our hearts. The Lord even challenges us to give so that we can see how faithful He really is. We read in Malachi 3:10 "Bring ye all the tithes into the storehouse, that there may be meat in mine house, and prove me now herewith, saith the LORD of hosts, if I will not open you the windows of heaven, and pour you out a blessing, that there shall not be room enough to receive it."

What we must remember is that everything begins with the seed. Whether it is a plant, a food or a human being, it all started with a seed. Before a farmer can harvest his fruits, vegetables or grains, he must first plant the appropriate seeds that will give him the harvest he needs. Then he must be diligent to fertilize, water and watch over his seeds to make sure they are healthy and growing in order to finally bring him his harvest. So it is with us. We are to sow our seeds with diligence and keep them watered with our prayers so when our harvest comes in, it will be well worth our wait.

I challenge you to be a giver in life. Sow your seeds consciously. Say kind words, do kind deeds, lift others up, and give from your whole heart so that God may be able to return it back to you multiplied many times over. Where should you give? Wherever it is needed. Give to your church, give to the ministry that feeds you spiritually, give to the shelters that help others, give to the places where you can see fruit coming forth from it. Give to the place that is blessed because that is good ground with good soil and will return to you a good harvest.

The wonderful thing about seeds is they multiply greatly when planted in good ground and the amount of harvest you receive is directly related to the amount of seeds that you've sown. The Bible declares in 2 Corinthians 9:6 "But this I say, He which soweth sparingly shall reap also sparingly; and he which soweth bountifully shall reap also bountifully." A farmer doesn't go looking for the harvest he never planted and it is the same with us. We shouldn't expect to reap in places where we've never planted. When we give cheerfully with an open heart, we can expect to receive the same in kind. A simple quote I love says "Givers gain". It may sound opposite to some, but the giver knows all too well how true it is. Be encouraged to try it for yourself and receive the blessing of being a giver. Always remember the one who gives the most also gains the most! (2 Corinthians 9:10-11)

Spending Time With The Lord

With the many pressures and stresses that we go through on a daily basis, we should remember where our strength and ability comes from. Thinking that we can do all things on our own will leave us exhausted and unable to handle the struggles that come our way. Only by surrendering to God and seeking that His will be done in our life can we be truly strengthened, encouraged and shown the right path for our life. How do we seek God's will? We do so by spending time alone with Him in prayer and we feel God speak to us by His Spirit when we read His Word. When we take the time to seek God for comfort, peace and strengthening, we are ensuring our success for our future. (2 Corinthians 12:9-10) (Proverbs 24:3-4)

The Lord is pleased when we seek Him. When our mind is focused on the Lord, He will give us peace that surpasses understanding. No matter what we go through and no matter what comes our way, we will not be moved or tempted to worry about anything. The Lord who holds us securely in His Hands will not let us go. He will protect us because our trust and faith lies solely in Him. When we tell God that our trust is in Him, that is when Heaven and Earth will move on your behalf. (Philippians 4:6-7) (Psalm 34:1-10)

Be encouraged to think on the Lord more. Spend time with Him in prayer, read your Bible more and allow the Holy Spirit to speak to you. Let God see your investment in Him. When we give all that we have to God and ask that He lead us onto the best path, we are showing the Lord that our trust lies solely in Him and that we trust in His divine plan for our life. No matter what comes your way, know that God loves you and wishes for you to commune with Him. Never forget that you are His beloved child and He loves you with an everlasting love. He wishes for you to be strengthened, encouraged, blessed and lifted up. Thank Him for all that He has given you in times past and seek to do His will all the days of your life. Doing so will ensure a blessed life. (Joshua 1:8-9) (Psalm 119:11-16)

Judgment And Condemnation - Why We Shouldn't Do It

In this world people are quick to bring condemnation and judgment against others either justifiably or wrongfully without taking into account their own sins and shortfalls. What we must both realize and recognize is that we are judge and jury over no one. God did not place us as individuals on the Earth to condemn or bring judgment against another. We are on this Earth to love the unlovable, forgive the unforgivable and lift up all those who are downtrodden. We are to offer a new beginning, a second chance, a clean slate and a fresh opportunity to all those who feel condemned, judged and accused. (Proverbs 18:8)

We who have been forgiven much should be quick to offer much forgiveness. We must remember the many times that we fell short whenever we are tempted to bring judgment against another. Just as we have received grace in our time of need from the Lord, we must also extend that same grace towards another. The Lord Jesus tells us in Matthew 5: 14-15 "For if ye forgive men their trespasses, your heavenly Father will also forgive you: But if ye forgive not men their trespasses, neither will your Father forgive your trespasses." Let us remember the words of the Lord and be quick to offer love and forgiveness.

So many people are quick to pull others down and bring judgment and condemnation against them, but let us separate ourselves and choose to act as Christ did. He forgave all who came to Him and cleansed them of their unrighteousness. He did not bring up their past, He did not bring requirements for them to meet to be forgiven. He forgave them without prejudice and asks us to do the same. A story that I think on concerning forgiveness is about the woman who was caught in the act of adultery. She was brought before Jesus by the "righteous men" of the city, the Scribes and Pharisees, and they proceeded to tell the Lord what she had done. After the Lord heard all that they had to say, He answered them very simply. Jesus said "He that is without sin among you, let him cast a stone at her." One by one they walked away because they were convicted in their conscience of their own sin. (John 8:1-11)

Let this message be an encouragement to you to never bring condemnation to another. Don't judge someone based on their past because in doing so, you may be hindering their future. We are not our past, but we are our future. Just because we have fallen short doesn't mean that is the end of the picture. A new beginning is possible to us as well as to those around us. If God forgave the woman who was caught in the act of adultery, He can also forgive all of us for our many shortfalls. For our lying, for our cheating, for our stealing, the blood of Jesus covers it all. He cleanses us of our unrighteousness and with His blood, we become cleaner than freshly fallen snow. Be encouraged again to encourage the discouraged and welcome in all those who felt the condemnation of others in times past. The Lord will be proud of you because you will act just as He did. (Leviticus 19:16) (Isaiah 1:18)

Sowing The Right Seeds

No matter where we are in life, we should expect to reap exactly what we sow. Whether we are happy and contented or discouraged and feeling miserable, if we think hard enough, we will find that our present reaping has much to do with how we sowed into our own lives. The Bible is a very accurate book and one needs only to look within its timeless pages to find the truths that are evident throughout. The Bible declares in Galatians 6:7-8 "Be not deceived; God is not mocked: for whatsoever a man soweth, that shall he also reap. For he that soweth to his flesh shall of the flesh reap corruption; but he that soweth to the Spirit shall of the Spirit reap life everlasting." (Psalm 119:10-16) (John 1:1-3) (Galatians 6:9-10)

We must think of our lives as living plants which will ultimately grow and show exactly the same types of seeds that were planted in our hearts. When we plant seeds of envy, jealousy, strife, hatred, etc., we shouldn't expect to reap generosity, love, peace and joy. We will receive or draw to ourselves exactly the same types of seeds that we have sown. We must remember this at all times and be mindful to carefully sow into our own lives and the lives of others good seeds that will bring back a good harvest of blessings. (2 Corinthians 9:6-9) (Luke 6:35-36) (Acts 20:35)

Message On Worshiping Only God

The Lord has spoken to my heart to write a message concerning how we should worship Him and how we should deal with the other Saints whom we also love. There are many people who truly love God, but have a misunderstanding concerning how they should pray and worship when it comes to the Saints of old. I hope this message truly ministers to your heart and shows you that only the Triune Godhead which is God the Father, God the Son and God the Holy Spirit is to be worshiped and exalted. (Isaiah 42:8) (Deut. 5:7-9; 6:13-15)

Concerning false worship, I think of the Virgin Mary. There are many people in the world who exalt the Virgin Mary even above the Lord Jesus Christ. They see her as holy because she gave birth to Jesus without ever knowing a man. While it is true that God favored her among women, the Bible never teaches that we should worship or pray to her. The Virgin Mary herself says in John 2:5 concerning Jesus "His mother saith unto the servants, Whatsoever He saith unto you, do it." We are to worship the Lord Jesus Christ. We are to pray to Him, seek His guidance and accept Him as our Lord and Savior because He is the one who died for our eternal Salvation. (Luke 1:28-30)

Concerning the other Saints such as Paul, Timothy, Luke, Mark and others that have become renowned through the centuries, we are to learn from what they have accomplished in their ministry for the Lord Jesus Christ, but we are not to pray to or worship them. The Bible says in 1 Timothy 2:5-6 "For there is one God, and One mediator between God and men, the man Christ Jesus; Who gave Himself a ransom for all, to be testified in due time." The Lord Jesus is enough. He is the One who died for us so that in the fullness of time we will be reconciled back to God the Father through Jesus. We are to worship Him, pray to Him, exalt Him and magnify Jesus above all others and let God know that our hearts are focused on Him. (Luke 1:34) (Luke 1:28) (Romans 5:10-11) (Psalm 115:1-18) (Isaiah 25:1)

How are we to pray? Should we pray to the Virgin Mary, to St. Paul or St. Timothy? Jesus made it very clear how we should pray. He never said to pray to a Saint or even to His mother. The Lord Jesus says in Matthew 6:9-13 "After this manner therefore pray ye: Our Father which art in heaven, Hallowed be thy name. Thy kingdom come. Thy will be done in earth, as it is in heaven. Give us this day our daily bread. And forgive us our debts, as we forgive our debtors. And lead us not into temptation, but deliver us from evil: For Thine is the kingdom, and the power, and the glory, for ever. Amen." As children of the Lord and followers of His command, we must take heed to follow what He has taught. We should not follow the traditions of men, but rather we are to follow the command of the Lord. (Exodus 20:3-5) (Jeremiah 29:13-14) (1 Chron. 16:29) (Isaiah 1:19)

To further show that only God in heaven is to be worshiped, I want to emphasize a couple of scriptures

195

from the Book of Revelation. When the Apostle John was caught up to heaven, he was amazed at all that he saw and when the angel had finished showing John the glories of heaven, John fell to his knees to worship the angel. We read this in Revelation 22:8-9 "I, John, am the one who heard and saw all these things. And when I heard and saw them, I fell down to worship at the feet of the angel who showed them to me. But he said, No, don't worship me. I am a servant of God, just like you and your brothers the prophets, as well as all who obey what is written in this book. Worship only God!" The Angel told the Apostle John that we are fellow workman for the Lord and only God is to be worshiped. The Angel dared not to accept worship and I believe the same would be said of all the Saints of old including the Virgin Mary. (Revelation 7:11; 19:10)

When we get to heaven on that glorious day there will not be denominational sections made in the kingdom of God. There won't be a Catholic section, a Baptist section, a Church of God section, a Pentecostal section, etc. In heaven, there will be the redeemed of the Lord Jesus Christ. Those who accepted Him as their Lord and Savior will be in heaven to worship the Lord God Jehovah. The same Saints that some of us pray to today will be on their knees just like the rest of us worshiping the God of heaven in truth and in humility. When God created the heavens and the earth, there was only the Triune Godhead in existence. Nobody else was there to help God or to give Him advice. He is the One we must worship. (Philippians 2:5-11)

I pray that you have received from this message what it was intended to impart. I mean no offense to anyone's denomination, but I do want to emphasize that the Bible is clear in how we must worship and pray to the Lord. If you are having trouble in this area of life, I encourage you to seek the Lord in prayer and ask for His guidance. The Lord is faithful to hear and answer your heartfelt prayer. (Romans 15:13-16) (Psalm 34:1-10)

Read and meditate on these scriptures:

Acts 4:12 "Neither is there salvation in any other: for there is none other name under Heaven given among men, whereby we must be saved."

John 3:16-18 Jesus declares "For God so loved the world, that He gave His only begotten Son, that whosoever believeth in Him should not perish, but have everlasting life. For God sent not His Son into the world to condemn the world; but that the world through Him might be saved. He that believeth on Him is not condemned: but he that believeth not is condemned already, because he hath not believed in the Name of the only begotten Son of God."

Psalm 116:1-2 "I love the LORD, because He hath heard my voice and my supplications. Because He hath inclined His ear unto me, therefore will I call upon Him as long as I live."

John 14:13-14 Jesus declares "And whatsoever ye shall ask in My name, that will I do, that the Father may be glorified in the Son. If ye shall ask any thing in My name, I will do it."

Revelation 11:16-17 "And the four and twenty elders, which sat before God on their seats, fell upon their faces, and worshipped God, Saying, We give Thee thanks, O Lord God Almighty, which art, and wast, and art to come; because Thou hast taken to Thee Thy great power, and hast reigned."

All of these scriptures can be found in the King James Version Bible.

Loving Yourself Enough

It is important to remember that God has created each of us as individuals with different gifts and talents which makes us unique. It is for this reason that we should love ourselves and use what God has given us for our betterment and not look at what others have in envy or jealousy. We who have trouble in this area of life must see our self-worth and know that God loves us just the way we are and has equipped us to stand in confidence and to reach forth towards victory. (Galatians 4:4-7) (Ephesians 1:4) (Jeremiah 31:3)

Be encouraged to love the person God made you to be. Never become envious or bitter when looking at what others possess, but rather stay faithful to the Lord and He will give you the desires of your heart. The Bible says it is God's good pleasure to give you the kingdom. Use what God has given you and love yourself enough to see that you are worthy of good things and that you are exactly what God had in mind when you were created. (Psalm 37:4) (Luke 12:32)

Encouraging Others By Example

The life that we lead is a living testimony to who we really are on the inside. Whether we realize it or not, people are watching to see how we carry ourselves in daily life. What we must always remember and keep in mind is that we should always act as Christ did and use our life as a living example to encourage, inspire and challenge all people to live life fully and be all that they were created to be. I can attest to the fact that it brings great joy to one's heart when they know their life has made an impact that will never be forgotten. (Luke 6:35-36)

When we take the initiative to encourage those who are feeling low and challenge those who feel like giving up to try just one more time, we are in essence acting as Angels in disguise. We are using our life to be a blessing in someone else's life and when we act in this manner, we are ensuring a blessed legacy. Be encouraged to live a life full of character, integrity and honor and use your life to make an impact on others that will never be erased or forgotten. (Galatians 6:9-10)

Message On Humility Before The Lord

The Lord has spoken to my heart to write a message on God's strength, our dependence on Him and our quiet confidence that all will be well. There is a story that I think on that shows how faithful the Lord is to those who depend on Him. The only thing God requires in return is our confession that He did it and not we ourselves. Humility before the Lord is greater than the riches of the world. The Bible declares in Psalm 100:3, "Know ye that the LORD He is God: it is He that hath made us, and not we ourselves; we are His people, and the sheep of His pasture." I hope this message on trusting and depending on the Lord encourages you to put on humility and lowliness of heart knowing that God is the One who brings victory and triumph into our lives. (Hebrews 12:28-29) (1 Peter 5:5-7) (1 Corinthians 15:57)

There is a story in the Old Testament about Gideon. Gideon was faithful to God and was used greatly by the Lord to defeat the enemies of Israel. It happened that God called Gideon to fight the armies of Midian. The armies of Midian had a total of a 135,000 trained warriors to fight against Israel. When Gideon gathered his army of warriors to fight the Midianites, Gideon's warriors totaled a number of 32,000 men. (Judges 6:12-14)

God spoke to Gideon and told him that he had too many fighters to fight the Midianites. God said if I allow you to use all these men to fight the Midianites, they will think that they defeated them with their own strength and not because I was with you. So God told Gideon to send those who were timid or afraid back to their homes. A total of 22,000 men returned home leaving only 10,000. Still God saw that they were too many and would be prideful and boastful when they defeated the Midianites. So another test that God told Gideon to do brought the number from 10,000 warriors down to 300 men. Now God was satisfied. He would use 300 men to defeat 135,000 Midianites to show that God is faithful to those who follow His command. (Judges 7:2-8)

When Gideon and his 300 men drew near to fight the Midianites, God caused confusion to come upon the Midianites and because of this, they turned on each other killing one another making it easy for Gideon and his warriors to defeat that vast army. Not one of Gideon's men died in that battle, but every single person from the Midianite army was killed. The Lord used just 300 men to defeat 135,000 men and showed all Israel how Mighty the Lord truly is. (Judges 7-8:23) (2 Chronicles 16:9) (Isaiah 50:2-10) (Exodus 4:11-12)

The point that I want to emphasize is that God wishes to fight our battles and lead us into victory. When we are weak, He is strong. When we are alone, He is our comforter. When we have no strength, He is our perfect strength. The Lord wishes to show Himself strong on behalf of those who trust Him. He is our encourager, helper, comforter, deliverer, director and Savior. There is no want in them that trust Him. The Lord Jehovah is everlasting strength. There is no weariness in Him and the

Lord never slumbers nor sleeps. Humble yourself before the Lord and confess with your mouth that you trust Him in everything and because you do victory will be yours. (2 Corinthians 12:9) (Psalm 34:22) (Psalm 121:1-8) (2 Chronicles 16:9)

Be encouraged to never be prideful or arrogant thinking that you can do it all. We are created from the dust of the earth and our life is as a vapor that is here today and gone tomorrow. Instead, boast in the Lord and in His goodness and know that those who give glory to God will never be left wanting, but will be filled with all good things for the remainder of their days. Praise the Lord for such goodness and mercy that is offered to all who humble themselves before Him and confess that He has made us what we are and not we ourselves. (1 Samuel 2:3) (Genesis 3:19) (Psalm 34:2)

Read and meditate on these scriptures:

Isaiah 42:8 "I am the LORD: that is My name: and My glory will I not give to another, neither My praise to graven images."

2 Chronicles 16:9 "For the eyes of the LORD run to and fro throughout the whole earth, to shew Himself strong in the behalf of them whose heart is perfect toward Him..."

Isaiah 1:18-19 "Come now, and let us reason together, saith the LORD: though your sins be as scarlet, they shall be as white as snow; though they be red like crimson, they shall be as wool. If ye be willing and obedient, ye shall eat the good of the land."

Proverbs 8:17-21 "I love them that love me; and those that seek me early shall find me. Riches and honour are with me; yea, durable riches and righteousness. My fruit is better than gold, yea, than fine gold; and my revenue than choice silver. I lead in the way of righteousness, in the midst of the paths of judgment: That I may cause those that love me to inherit substance; and I will fill their treasures."

All of these scriptures can be found in the King James Version Bible.

Leading A Faith Filled Life

There are many moments in life when we are tempted to worry and fear what the future holds. Whether we receive a bad report about our health, our job or our finances, we should address it with faith and confidence. We shouldn't become hysterical and allow fear to take root in our hearts because the Lord who has created all things is still in control of our lives. Those who depend on Him already know that God sees the end result of the path that they're still traveling on. Nothing can take God by surprise and if we who depend on Him act in a manner that is less than trusting than how can we expect God to faithfully meet our needs. What we must remember is that faith is our greatest asset and that's the only thing that pleases God. The Bible says that without faith it is impossible to please God because he who comes to God must believe that He is and that He is a rewarder of those who diligently seek Him. (Psalm 46:1-5) (Hebrews 11:6)

Faith is what we hold on to until the answer comes. The word faith is defined in Hebrews 11:1 like this "Faith is the substance of things hoped for, the evidence of things not seen." When we pray in faith and ask God to meet our needs, we should not stop asking until that need has been met. That is when faith manifests itself. The Lord Jesus tells us to ask, seek and knock. I believe the Lord wants us to pray in triplicate because He doesn't want us to give up when the answer doesn't come immediately or as we had hoped it would. We must remember that God is omnipotent, omniscient, and omnipresent which means He is all powerful and knows all things at all times in all places. There is nothing too hard for the Lord, but we must trust Him and have faith that our needs will be met. Be encouraged to trust the Lord with your life. He loves you more than you'll ever know and wishes to lead your life on to the best path. When we depend on Him, our hearts can rest confidently because the Lord will never fail His beloved child. (Psalm 118:6-9) (Matthew 7:7-9)

Blessing Our Relationships

Our relationships are the most important thing in our lives, but many times we forget how much our loved ones mean to us and we end up taking them for granted. We may treat them harshly, not consider their feelings or simply not be there for them when they need us. What we must realize is that those we love the most also deserve our attention the most. We cannot ignore their needs and just be around when it's convenient for us, but rather we have to be there when they need us. Whether it is our parent, spouse or our children, we need to be there to nurture those relationships and make our love known. I know of many people who neglect those closest to them and in the end they pay a price for doing so. They don't realize the damage they are doing by not paying attention to those closest to them until it is too late. What they would have quickly found is that doing simple things like giving and receiving in conversation, being courteous with one another and simply making an effort can do so much to show our loved ones that we care. (Hebrews 13:1-3) (1 John 4:7-11)

What we must remember is that anything neglected will eventually die. Whether it is something as simple as a plant or something as complicated as the human body, if it is not taken care of, it will perish. It is the same thing with our relationships. Just like a plant, our relationships also need to be fed, watered, pruned, given enough sunlight and shown a little tender loving care. When it is, it will flourish and last a lifetime. Let us realize this truth and see that our family and friends need us as much as we need them. Be encouraged to reevaluate how you are spending your time and if changes need to be made, make them quickly. Spend time with those who mean the most to you. Realize that they need you as much as you need them. When you do, great things will begin to take place in both of your lives.

Storing Up Treasures...

We should always remember and keep in perspective that this life is temporary. As long as it may seem right now while we are going through it, it will pass us by all too quickly and we will wonder where the time went. Life when compared to eternity is like a drop of water in an ocean. The brevity of life should make us more focused on our eternity and building on goodwill that will bring us rewards when we get to our home in heaven. Many times we focus so much on attaining physical possessions and building our wealth on the Earth while the lack any thought of building treasures in heaven. The Lord Jesus knew of this wrongful thinking that many people had even in His day and declared in Matthew 6:19-21 "Lay not up for yourselves treasures upon earth, where moth and rust doth corrupt, and where thieves break through and steal: But lay up for yourselves treasures in heaven, where neither moth nor rust doth corrupt, and where thieves do not break through nor steal: For where your treasure is, there will your heart be also." What our eyes and mind is focused on is where our heart and soul will move towards. (Malachi 3:10-12) (James 4:14)

Let us remember to build up our treasures in heaven. Let us do good works, help others in need, be someone's shoulder to lean upon, encourage and lift up those who are feeling low and simply be an example of the same love that Christ showed when He was on the Earth. We are His ambassadors and He calls us to move in His stead teaching His principles and leading others to His saving grace. We who have given our lives to the Lord should strive to live, breathe and act in a manner that is pleasing to Him so that when we see the Lord on that glorious day, we will have been proud of how we carried ourselves while we were alive on the Earth. Be encouraged to lead by example, live with integrity and help to make better every life that comes across your path. Doing so will ensure treasures untold prepared for you in heaven. (2 Corinthians 5:20-21) (Romans 12:9-13)

Asking For Help When We Need It

There are many people in this world who are lost. They may be lost spiritually, lost in their professional career, lost in their relationships and they don't know how to get back on the right track. What we must all realize is that we are all fallible and will be in need of assistance at some point in our lives. We will never have all the answers to life's problems, but if we have a humble heart and seek help, most times the answer to our dilemma is not far away. (1 Corinthians 10:12) (1 Peter 5:6-7)

What keeps most people from seeking help is their arrogance, pride or ego. People don't want to seem weak and if they admit to someone else that they are lacking in a certain area, they believe that others will look down upon them and see them as less than. What they must realize is that feeling lost at some point in our lives is normal. We will not always have the answer to life's problems, but others who have already gone down our path may be able to help us become better, wiser and stronger than we were before. Having a humble heart and realizing that it's okay to ask for help is what elevates us to the heights of victory in our life. Realizing that we're not perfect may help us to seek help quicker and in doing so, bring the answer quicker as well. (Psalm 138:6) (Proverbs 4:20-23)

No matter what you're going through in life, know that you can ask for help. Whether it is asking God through prayer, seeking counsel from a pastor, asking your spouse, your parent, your siblings or a professional. The first step is recognizing that we have a problem and need help to resolve it. The second step is knowing that it's okay to seek help so that we may become better quicker and the third and most difficult step is swallowing our pride and seeking help from someone who can resolve our issue. What we will quickly find is that others are eager to help when we simply ask for it. Confiding in someone else and admitting that we need help brings about compassion, empathy and love and those ingredients can do so much to make a bad situation so much better. (Proverbs 1:5) (Proverbs 11:14)

Be encouraged to seek help when you're feeling lost. Whatever the issue may be, know that you can overcome it and become better in the end because of it. Never think that you are weak because you need help. Asking for help makes you stronger than you can ever know and overcoming that issue will make you feel on top of the world. Don't keep holding it in when help is so close to you. The Bible says that we are to ask, seek and knock and when we do the door will be opened to us. I encourage you to follow that same advice and ask, seek and knock until you find the answers that you are looking for. (Matthew 7:7-8)

Message On Sowing And Reaping

I have been meditating on a verse of scripture for the past few weeks and the Lord has really been speaking to my heart about it. The scripture is in Galatians 6:7 "Be not deceived; God is not mocked: for whatsoever a man soweth, that shall he also reap." Many people think that they can go through life and cheat, steal and lie and never have to pay a price for their life of sin, but this scripture is a big warning to every person that whatever you do, it will come back to you.

I think about sowing and reaping a lot because it is amazing to me how true it is. Whatever you put into the ground whether it be physical or spiritual will grow and come back to you one day. If we were to plant tomato seeds into the ground, we cannot expect strawberries to grow and if we were to plant an apple tree, we can't expect oranges to grow. It's the same thing in life; if we sow hatred, bitterness, strife, and deceit, then we shouldn't expect to reap; love, peace and joy. The laws of God work the same both in the physical and spiritual realm. What ever we put into the ground will mature and grow and come back to either bless or curse our life.

I encourage you to always remind yourself of this scripture and get it deep in your spirit. Whatever you sow, that is what you are going to reap. Be quick to help someone in need and say good things about others even when you're tempted to do otherwise. Give, help, and bless others; not to look for a reward from those people, but because God Almighty will bless and reward you in like manner. Always remember there is a whole world that we cannot see and God's angels are writing down all that we do; in secret and openness (Malachi 3:13-18).

If people do bad things to you, repay them with good. If people talk bad about you; you in turn say something good about them. God is watching and His judgment is just. God Himself said vengeance is mine so let God be God and you do all you can in repaying good for evil. (Romans 12:19) (Deuteronomy 32:35)

I hope you will take this message to heart and allow the Lord to work in your life in every area that you are lacking. I encourage you to call upon the Lord and ask Him to help you to be more alert concerning sowing and reaping. I thank the Lord for putting this scripture on my heart and He will do the same for you if you ask Him because God is no respecter of persons (Acts 10:34).

Read and meditate on these scriptures:

Galatians 6:7-8 "Be not deceived; God is not mocked: for whatsoever a man soweth, that shall he also reap. For he that soweth to his flesh shall of the flesh reap corruption; but he that soweth to the Spirit shall of the Spirit reap life everlasting."

Romans 12:19-21 "Dearly beloved, avenge not yourselves, but rather give place unto wrath: for it is written,

Vengeance is mine; I will repay, saith the Lord. Therefore if thine enemy hunger, feed him; if he thirst, give him drink: for in so doing thou shalt heap coals of fire on his head. Be not overcome of evil, but overcome evil with good."

Matthew 5:8-12 Jesus says "Blessed are the pure in heart: for they shall see God. Blessed are the peacemakers: for they shall be called the children of God. Blessed are they which are persecuted for righteousness' sake: for theirs is the kingdom of heaven. Blessed are ye, when men shall revile you, and persecute you, and shall say all manner of evil against you falsely, for my sake. Rejoice, and be exceeding glad: for great is your reward in heaven: for so persecuted they the prophets which were before you."

Romans 12:14-17 "Bless them which persecute you: bless, and curse not. Rejoice with them that do rejoice, and weep with them that weep. Be of the same mind one toward another. Mind not high things, but condescend to men of low estate. Be not wise in your own conceits. Recompense to no man evil for evil. Provide things honest in the sight of all men."

All scriptures can be found in the King James Version.

Not Expecting The World

We should always remember and keep in mind that in life we will have good days and bad days, ups and downs, happiness and sadness, lots of laughter and sometimes many tears. We should never expect to always be above in life. Thinking that the good times will last forever will inevitably bring disappointment because when the hard times come our way, we will find our joy replaced with discouragement and sadness. Instead, we should take each day as it comes and be appreciative for the blessing of that day. Just as we don't expect the sun to always be shining on us, we should have that same mind set for ourselves as well as for others. (Ecclesiastes 3:1-8) (Nehemiah 8:10)

Expectations bring disappointment because when someone doesn't do what we wanted them to do, then our perception of them changes. If they didn't meet a deadline, if they didn't meet a certain need, if they didn't say the right thing, etc. When we expect much, we leave ourselves open for disillusionment, distress and many times we are letdown. Accepting others for who they are and allowing them to surprise us is where we should be in our relationships.

Doing our best at a certain task and accepting the results helps us to excel just the same because our expectations were not held at such an unreachable level. Doing our best at a professional level and at a personal level is all we should expect of ourselves as well as from those whom we love. Be encouraged to never place labels on what you want people to do or to be. Accept them for who they are and love them right where they are. That will ensure blessed relationships and will eliminate unneeded stress in both of your lives. (Proverbs 10:12)

Have Faith In God

It is important in life that we continually stand strong and show our confidence in God's ability to strengthen us, meet our needs and deliver us from the obstacles that come our way. The Lord declares in Psalm 46:10 "Be still, and know that I am God..." The Lord is able to do exceeding abundantly above all that we ask or think and we are to remember to be still and know that God's Spirit is right by our side. Isaiah 59:1 says, "Behold, the Lord's hand is not shortened, that it cannot save; neither His ear heavy, that it cannot hear." God is the faithful Father who promised to never leave you, but will hear your prayer and save you with His mighty hand. (Ephesians 3:20)

We should never allow worry or anxiety to enter into our hearts and keep us from reaching the heights of victory that God wishes for us to reach and stand upon. The Lord is our strength and refuge as we read in Psalm 46:1 "God is our refuge and strength, a very present help in trouble." Be encouraged to continue on and know that God is with you and will meet your every need because of your faith, confidence and trust in Him. (Psalm 37:3-9)

Asking For God's Strengthening

When life gets overwhelming as it sometimes does, it is important that we come before the Lord asking for His strength and sustenance to take over where ours has been spent. God in His infinite grace and mercy is ready and willing to lift us up when we are feeling low and strengthen us when we have no strength left. The Lord knows our frame and remembers that we are mere dust formed by His perfect molding hands. It is okay for us to recognize our weakness and confess that we need His intervention. The Bible says that God resists the proud, but He gives Grace to the humble. (Psalm 46:1-3)

We are all in need of His grace and when difficult times come before us, we can rest knowing that God's infinite grace isn't far away. Remember that He loves you and died for you and wishes for your Joy to be full. Rest in the Lord and know that He has perfect strength to sustain you and keep you all the days of your life. (Isaiah 26:3-4) (Psalm 103:13-14) (1 Peter 5:5)

Getting Past Old Hurts

Many times we allow our past hurts and heartbreaks to keep us from trusting again and from living life to its fullest potential. What we must realize is that no person will escape being hurt in this life. It is all a part of living and being alive. As long as we have breath in our lungs, we should expect to get hurt at some point in our lives, but getting hurt should not keep us stagnant in life. Just because we have suffered heartbreak does not mean that we should give up on all people and not allow ourselves to trust again. Life is all about second chances. God offers second chances to us so we should also give ourselves a second chance to live life to its fullest potential. That entails getting past what has happened to us and using it for our benefit to become better, wiser and stronger than we were before. (Philippians 3:13-14)

We must always keep in mind that past hurts can do two things; they can make us bitter or they can make us better. We can either become stagnant and stay in that negative state of mind, or we can rise up, learn from that situation and use our life to be a blessing to ourselves as well as to those around us. Be encouraged and know that your heart has a resilience like none other. The Lord can heal every brokenness that our hearts have suffered and give us a strength that we never thought was possible. Do all that you can to move your life in a positive direction using all that you have learned and experienced to better your life and don't be afraid to trust again. You may have suffered at one time, but your latter end is sure to be much brighter and much more victorious than any of the former miseries that came your way in times past. Trust God, stay faithful to Him and you will see His favour poured over your life. (1 Peter 5:10-11) (Psalm 61:1-4)

Know That Good Will Come Again

When life seems overwhelming as it sometimes does, we should remember to keep things in perspective. Many times we focus so much on the bad that we are currently going through that we don't take time to realize how temporary that situation is. We must remember that in life we will experience all emotions. We will have good times and bad, laughter and tears, happiness and sadness, feelings of optimism and pessimism and moments of triumph and despair. We will experience all of these emotions in life, but what we must always remember is that the good times will greatly outweigh the bad. We just have to be steady and know to be patient because whatever bad is trying to discourage our hearts will soon pass away. Never give in to those negative feelings even if life seems too much to handle in that moment. Life is never too much to handle because God is able to take our heavy burden and ease it with His gentle Spirit. (2 Corinthians 4:15-18) (Jeremiah 31:13)

All we have to do is simply call upon the Lord and ask for His ever-present help. The Bible declares in Psalm 103:8 "The Lord is merciful and gracious, slow to anger, and plenteous in mercy." The Lord is our strong tower and our solid rock. He is our portion for peace even when everything else around us is crumbling. The Lord can restore unto us peace like we've never felt so let us remember His goodness and know that life can be lived to the full if only we keep our remembrance that the good times will come again and will greatly overshadow any bad that came our way in times past. Be encouraged to remember to have a proper perspective if you are going through a rough time right now. It will get better; that is a guaranteed promise. Just be patient and know that great things will soon come your way. (Psalm 46:1-4) (Psalm 61:1-3) (Proverbs 18:10)

Last Night I Dreamed of Jesus

In my dream, I was suddenly in Heaven and the first thought I had was about my dad. I wanted to see my dad who passed away in February 2001, but something told me no. I don't know if it was my own mind or the Holy Spirit, I'm not sure, but something told me "You have to see Jesus first." Then just that quick I was brought to Jesus. I don't remember anybody leading me to Him or anybody taking me to where He was, I was just suddenly standing before Him. I don't remember focusing on anything except His face. Then He spoke to me. He said, "Dwayne thank you for proclaiming my name so well, thank you for telling others about me, thank you for always lifting my name so high." The last thing He said to me was "I am proud of you."

Those are the only things I remember Jesus saying to me, but the look in His eyes is something that was equally as beautiful or even more beautiful. The look in His eyes said to me "I know you, I've known you, and I've seen everything you've been through." His look was so pleasing, so beautiful, so peaceful. That is something that will stick with me for a long time. I never said anything to Him. I don't remember speaking. I'm not sure why, but I didn't. When I opened my eyes, I didn't feel like I was dreaming. It felt real. It felt like I was having a vision with my eyes closed. That was amazing to me.

This is the second time I've seen the Lord Jesus. The first time was almost 17 years ago. It was about a month after my boating accident and I was still at the rehab center. In my dream, the Lord came to my bedside and stood beside me. He placed His right hand over my heart and without speaking I felt Him say to me "I will give you peace." And then I woke up. Looking back on that dream now, I am thankful for His grace. The reason is because I wasn't a Christian at that time. I didn't accept the Lord as my savior until a year after that dream. The Lord has been faithful. He has given me peace that is comforting. He has given me wisdom beyond my years, mercy for the times I fall short, and grace to carry my burden with a peace that surpasses all understanding.

The Lord is faithful even when we fall short. His mercy reaches from everlasting to everlasting. His love knows no end and His forgiveness is without limit. The Lord is worthy of our praise. I have dedicated my life to Him and I pray that many will receive for themselves the peace, love and forgiveness that Jesus Christ offers to all who call upon His Name. He is the King of Kings and Lord of Lords and is worthy to receive our praise.

I am thankful.

–Dwayne

Written on May 23, 2011

Copyright

<u>Feedback</u>

When I am reading a book and find a typo, I find it distracting and it takes my focus off of the message. That is why I would ask that if you find any kind of formatting errors or typos in the messages that you would contact me and let me know of the error so that it can be corrected in an updated edition of this book.

You can report any errors directly through the Kindle device that you are using or you can send a direct email to Messagesofhope@outlook.com

I greatly appreciate any help or feedback that you may be able to give.

–Dwayne

Review Request

Thank you so much for taking the time to read the messages in this book. If you have a couple of minutes I humbly ask that you write a review for this book on Amazon.com.

I believe book reviews are an important part in letting others know that a book is worthy to be read, how it impacted the reader and what others can expect to gain from that book.

I don't have a marketing campaign or hired help to promote the book and that is why I ask for the reader to let others know of how they too could be blessed by the messages available in this book.

Thank you for your time. I really do appreciate it.

–Dwayne

Made in the USA
Charleston, SC
06 December 2014